The

JOURNEY

to

PEACE

IMAGE BOOKS / DOUBLEDAY

New York London Toronto Sydney Auckland

The

JOURNEY

to

PEACE

Reflections on Faith,

Embracing Suffering,

and Finding New Life

JOSEPH CARDINAL

BERNARDIN

SELECTIONS, INTRODUCTIONS, AND PRAYERS
BY ALPHONSE P. SPILLY, C.PP.S.,
AND JEREMY LANGFORD

AN IMAGE BOOK

PUBLISHED BY DOUBLEDAY

a division of Random House, Inc.

IMAGE, DOUBLEDAY, and the portrayal of a deer drinking from a
stream are registered trademarks of Random House, Inc.

Book design by Pei Loi Koay
Illustrations by Margaret Chodos-Irvine

The Library of Congress has cataloged the Doubleday hardcover
edition as follows:
Bernardin, Joseph Louis, 1928–
The journey to peace: reflections on faith, embracing suffering, and
finding new life/Joseph Cardinal Bernardin; selections and
introductions by Alphonse P. Spilly and Jeremy Langford.— 1st ed.
p.   cm.
Includes bibliographical references.
1. Bernardin, Joseph Louis, 1928–   2. Cardinals—Illinois—
Chicago Region—Biography.   3. Catholic Church—Illinois—
Chicago Region—Biography.   4. Chicago Region (Ill.)—Church
history—20th century.   5. Death—Religious aspects—Catholic
Church.   6. Spiritual life—Catholic Church.   I. Title.

BX4705.B38125 A3 2001
252'.02—dc21
00-063929

ISBN 0-385-50102-1

PRINTED IN THE UNITED STATES OF AMERICA

First Image Books Edition: February 2003

3   5   7   9   10   8   6   4   2

CONTENTS

PREFACE

When Cardinal Joseph Bernardin died on November 14, 1996, people around the globe mourned his passing. In Chicago, where Bernardin had served as archbishop since 1982, nearly 200,000 people of all ages, backgrounds and faiths, formed a continuous line around Holy Name Cathedral for forty-two hours to view the cardinal's body lying in state and say good-bye. Bernardin's funeral, televised across America and beyond, drew together leaders from many religions, dignitaries, clergy, religious, parishioners, family and friends. All those in attendance and tuning in from afar celebrated the cardinal's earthly life and his passing into life eternal.

Following the funeral, thousands of us lined State Street outside the cathedral as the cortege prepared for its long, slow journey west through the city to Mount Carmel Cemetery in Hillside, Illinois, where Cardinal Bernardin was entombed that evening. As the pallbearers placed the cardinal's casket inside the hearse and those in the procession climbed into their cars and broke the awed silence with the closing of their doors, a woman behind us whispered to her friend, "What are we looking at? Help me place this event. What have we had in our midst?"

The friend replied, scanning the crowd, "A very special man."

Joseph Bernardin was a very special man indeed. He had always taken his priesthood, prayer life, spirituality and pastoral ministry very seriously. From the time he was diagnosed as having pancreatic cancer in June 1995 until he died in November 1996, he was often asked what he hoped to accomplish with his remaining time on earth. Bernardin made it clear that he had lived a full life and that, because he had focused on the essentials, he was not racing to make up for lost time. He explained that the greatest witness of his faith, the best sermon he could ever give, would be the way he lived out the rest of his life.

It was.

Ever the consummate minister, Cardinal Bernardin spent the final months of his life tirelessly reaching out to cancer patients and the terminally ill by praying with and for them, making personal visits, writing letters, and talking on the telephone. Though his cancer had gone into remission after surgery and treatment soon after it was diagnosed, he began to experience excruciating pain from spinal stenosis and the eventual collapse of four vertebrae. Yet his will to serve allowed him to transform his pain into deeper compassion for and commitment to those who needed him most. Up until two weeks before his death he continued to serve as Archbishop of Chicago, visiting parishes, speaking out against partial-birth abortion and physician-assisted suicide, helping to found the Catholic Common Ground Initiative and maintaining his communications with people of all ages who wanted to learn from his faith and his example.

Cardinal Bernardin took to heart Saint James's admonition "Faith without works is dead." The son of Italian immigrants, Bernardin was instilled from youth with a strong work ethic. He viewed life as a precious gift and nurtured his relationship with God, the source of all, so that he could receive life, be life and share life with others. He truly believed that actions speak louder than words.

Yet among the many gifts of this special man was the ability to put his actions and convictions into words. A skilled speaker and writer, Bernardin carefully crafted his homilies, lectures, prayers, pastoral letters, press conferences, reports to Rome and personal correspondence. His obvious passion for the Word of God honed his keen sense of the power of words to touch people's lives and open their minds, hearts and souls to the gospel message.

When on August 28, 1996, Cardinal Bernardin was told by his doctors that his cancer had returned after fifteen months of being in remission and that it was terminal, he did what he always had done when there was important news to share: He called a press conference. Standing before a crowded roomful of reporters only two days after hearing the news from his doctors, he explained that his cancer had spread to his liver, that he was going to try a new form of chemotherapy, and that he had to cancel his previously planned back surgery intended to relieve the pain along his spine.

In a remarkably personal moment, the cardinal said, "Over the past year I have counseled the cancer patients with whom I have been in touch . . . to place themselves entirely in the hands of the Lord. I have personally always tried to do that; now I have done so with greater conviction and trust than ever before. While I know that, humanly speaking, I will have to deal with difficult moments, I can say in all sincerity that I am at peace. I consider this as God's special gift to me at this moment in my life."

In the last months of his life, Cardinal Bernardin made it his mission to share his personal reflections and insights, most specifically by writing a book called *The Gift of Peace*. Using as a framework the last three years of his life—years that included a false accusation of sexual misconduct, which ended in a profound act of forgiveness and reconciliation with his accuser; the diagnosis of cancer and subsequent period of remission; and the return of the cancer and the freeing process of letting go and befriending death—the cardinal invited people to walk with him the final miles of his life's journey. He invited them to share in God's gift to us all, the gift of peace.

Released two months after his death, *The Gift of Peace* became a national bestseller and remained so for over four months. It has appeared in twelve foreign editions, reaching across geographic, racial, ethnic and religious boundaries.

WE WERE BOTH PROFOUNDLY PRIVILEGED to work with Cardinal Bernardin on *The Gift of Peace*.

And we remain dedicated to preserving his legacy by making his thought as widely available as possible.

Soon after Cardinal Bernardin's death, the idea for this book was born. The cardinal had reached people by sharing his story, his struggles, his faith and his acceptance of God's gift of peace. But he also left us all wanting more.

Being as prolific and organized as he was, by the time of his death Cardinal Bernardin's archives included over fifteen hundred homilies. As we thought of ways to organize selections from a portion of these homilies into a book, it became clear that the Stations of the Cross provided a very appropriate framework. Bernardin himself had used the Stations to enter more deeply into the mystery of Jesus' suffering, death and resurrection. He believed that the Stations help us all to walk with Jesus and recognize that Jesus walks with us through this life and into the next.

Though he did not write or preach precisely about the Stations themselves, his words often illuminated aspects of Jesus' suffering, death and resurrection in new and timely ways. In March 1995 Cardinal Bernardin made a historic trip to the Holy Land and walked the Way of the Cross in person with an interfaith delegation of Jews and Catholics. The event touched him deeply, walking where his Savior had walked on the journey to Calvary. For the cardinal, the journey with Jesus is truly the journey to peace and freedom.

The Journey to Peace: Reflections on Faith, Embracing Suffering, and Finding New Life offers previously unpublished selections from over thirty of Cardinal Bernardin's homilies that help us enter more fully into the mystery of Jesus the Christ. They also help us deepen our own faith on the journey to peace and freedom as we understand how Bernardin, a man of great consistency and integrity, came to accept God's gift of peace over the course of his lifetime.

THIS BOOK HAS BEEN IN the making for nearly four years and could not have come into being without the help of a small group of people who believed in it from the start. We are grateful to Bishop Raymond Goedert, longtime friend of Cardinal Bernardin and vicar general of the Archdiocese of Chicago, for granting permission to use the excerpts from Bernardin's homilies, thus making this book possible; to Cardinal Francis George, Archbishop of Chicago, for so graciously honoring and preserving his predecessor's legacy; to John White, Pulitzer Prize–winning photojournalist, who captured the essence of his dear friend in his photo biographies *This Man Bernardin* and *The Final Journey of*

Joseph Cardinal Bernardin, for teaching us all to see the divine in the ordinary; and to Monsignor Kenneth Velo; Sister Mary Brian Costello, R.S.M., and Reverends Louis Cameli, Francis Kane, Michael Place and Robert Schreiter, C.P.P.S., who have served as valuable consultants on all the publications of Cardinal Bernardin's works.

AND FINALLY WE THANK THE people of Doubleday, who keep *The Gift of Peace* in print and who warmly embraced this project. Senior editor Trace Murphy brought both projects to Doubleday and edited *The Journey to Peace* with rare grace and skill. Publisher Eric Major's enthusiasm for such projects is legendary, and we thank him for adding this one to his fine list.

—Alphonse P. Spilly, C.PP.S., and Jeremy Langford

EDITORS'

INTRODUCTION

Joseph Louis Bernardin was born in Columbia, South
Carolina, on April 2, 1928. Although he began a premed
program at the University of South Carolina, within a
year he had decided to enter the seminary instead. He
was ordained to the priesthood for the Diocese of
Charleston in 1952. After serving that diocese for fourteen years in a variety of roles, he was appointed auxil-
iary bishop of the Archdiocese of Atlanta in 1966, just
months after the Second Vatican Council ended. The
youngest bishop in the country at the time, Bishop
Bernardin found in Archbishop Paul Hallinan his first
important mentor. Hallinan was enthusiastic about the

reforms of the council, and Bishop Bernardin followed closely in his footsteps.

In 1968 Bernardin was elected the general secretary of the U.S. episcopal conference and found his second important mentor, John Cardinal Dearden, Archbishop of Detroit and president of the episcopal conference. During the four years that Bernardin served in Washington, D.C., he played a major role in reorganizing the episcopal conference according to the norms of the Second Vatican Council. He also earned a reputation as a reconciler, a person who could listen to all sides of an argument and help people find common ground.

In 1972 Pope Paul VI appointed Bernardin Archbishop of Cincinnati, and during Bernardin's ten years there he also served a three-year term as president of the U.S. Catholic bishops' conference.

In 1982 Pope John Paul II appointed him Archbishop of Chicago, where he served with distinction until his death. Bernardin was elevated to the College of Cardinals in February 1983, and his love and concern for the Church throughout the world became widely known and respected.

But it was Joseph Bernardin the man of faith who is remembered by most people. He was a holy and human person. He had an uncanny ability to talk about his personal journey of faith and the struggles he encountered along the way. He did not spend all of his time at prayer, however. While he devoted the first hour of each day to prayer, he was a bishop after the model of the Good Shepherd, dealing boldly and confidently with modern-day problems.

He chaired the U.S. Catholic bishops' ad hoc committee that drafted a national pastoral letter on war and peace, which eventually received the nearly unanimous support of the bishops. In connection with this project, his portrait appeared on the cover of *Time* magazine. In 1983 he began to articulate the need for a consistent ethic of life, linking all the life issues—from conception to natural death—even though he recognized that each of the life issues was also distinct and needed separate analysis. He was very much at home in ecumenical and interfaith dialogue. In fact, he so distinguished himself in Catholic-Jewish dialogue that the Jewish community of metropolitan Chicago held a prayer service in Holy Name Cathedral before his funeral rites. He took a keen interest in Catholic health care, and his concerns deepened when he became a cancer patient himself.

He announced the Catholic Common Ground Initiative in mid August 1996, only two weeks before he discovered that his cancer had returned and was terminal. On September 9 he was awarded the Presidential Medal of Freedom, the nation's highest civilian honor, for being a bridge builder and showing us that life is too precious to waste on division and acrimony. And during the ten weeks or so that remained of his life, he taught all of us how to die, as *Newsweek* magazine pointed out a few days after his death in a lead story that featured a picture of the late, beloved cardinal on the magazine's cover.

Cardinal Bernardin was not afraid to live, and therefore he did not fear death. He took risks when necessary and was willing to pay the price for the positions he took. Above all, as he pointed out at his installation as Archbishop of Chicago, he modeled his episcopal ministry on that of the Good Shepherd and was willing to lay down his life for his flock. He had no illusions about what this meant. He had often prayed the mysteries of the Rosary and had walked with his Lord in the Stations of the Cross. He had an intimate knowledge of the Cross in his own life—and recognized it in others' lives—but he was always a man of hope, because he believed that God will never abandon his people. In the darkest moments the cardinal would affirm that somehow, with God's help, new life comes out of pain and suffering.

AMONG THE OLDEST AND MOST familiar Catholic devotional exercises, the Stations of the Cross date as far back as patristic antiquity and gained in popularity throughout the Middle Ages. Originally pilgrims would physically journey to Jerusalem and visit the various sites associated with Christ's suffering and death. But because most people could not make such a pilgrimage, over time there grew a demand for pictorial representations of the last events in Jesus' life. By the twelfth century the fervor of the Crusades and a heightened devotion to the Passion created a heavy demand for such pictorial representations.

When the Franciscans took over custody of the shrines in the Holy Land in 1342, they viewed it as part of their mission to propagate what came to be known as Stations of the Cross, or the Way of the Cross. Though many saints were devoted to the Way of the Cross, perhaps no one did more to promote it than Saint Leonard of Port Maurice, Italy (1676–1751). As a Franciscan priest, Saint Leonard preached the Way of the Cross at missions and reportedly set up Stations in 571 locations throughout Italy. Early on, there was no consensus as to the number and title of these Stations, but by the eighteenth century a series of papal pronouncements set the number at fourteen. In recent times liturgists and many others, including Pope John Paul II, have emphasized a need for a "Fifteenth Station" that depicts the resurrection.

Using the Stations of the Cross as a framework, *The Journey to Peace* offers previously unpublished excerpts from Cardinal Bernardin's homilies that can be used to reflect on various aspects of each Station. With the cardinal as our guide, *The Journey to Peace* asks us to put ourselves fully in God's presence and to journey with his Son each step of the way on the road to and from the tomb. Cardinal Bernardin was himself a pilgrim, and he fully understood that making a pilgrimage is never easy. When we set out on a journey, there is always a sense of displacement, imbalance, mystery, and even fear that goes with moving from the familiar to the unknown. For Christians, the incarnation, suffering, death and resurrection of Jesus the Christ are at the very heart of the mystery we enter into as pilgrims of faith. If we were ever asked by Jesus, as Peter was, "Who do you say that I am?" how would we respond? As believers, each of us is called to find the answer by journeying with Jesus as he breaks open radically new and intimate ways of being in relationship with God, transforms the law, heals the sick, comforts the afflicted, shows mercy to even the worst of sinners, breaks bread with the marginalized and teaches us how to be who God calls us to be.

We are also called to be Christ's disciples in the modern world. When we make the Way of the Cross, we are not being morbid, nostalgic or locked in the past. Quite the contrary! We are studying the very foundation of our faith, upon which we are called to build the kingdom of God on earth. Unless we embrace the Cross, we cannot embrace the resurrection. It is that simple. And that profound.

As you read this book, we invite you to stop, to meditate on each Station and all that it tells you about Jesus and about yourself as one of his followers. Why was Jesus sentenced to death? What did it mean for him to bear his cross—the instrument of his death? How was he able to fall and get up three different times? What was it like for Jesus to meet his mother while being mocked and scorned? What is the significance of Jesus' accepting help from Simon of Cyrene and receiving such gentle compassion from Veronica, only to turn around and tell the women of Jerusalem not to weep for him? What was it like for Jesus to be stripped of his clothes and dignity, nailed to a cross, buried and then raised from the dead? And what does each of these events mean for us today?

Our prayer and hope is that as you read this book in portions throughout the year, you will accept Cardinal Bernardin's invitation to enter more deeply into the mystery of Jesus' Passion and resurrection and find yourself further along the road on your own journey to peace.

INVITATION TO
A JOURNEY

Each of us journeys in this life from birth to death. God has chosen a path for us and calls us to walk along it. But he has also created us with free will and allows us to follow a route of our own choosing. There is nothing more important than choosing a path that leads to meaning, fulfillment, compassion and joy. If we choose our own path, we risk the consequences of walking alone, with only our own meager resources. But if we choose to walk in God's ways, he will give us all we need for the journey. When there are forks in the road, obstacles to be overcome or alternate routes to take, God accompanies us and helps us discern his path from others.

Wherever our journey of faith takes us, it inevitably

encounters suffering. Our culture, to the contrary, tells us to avoid suffering at all cost. Advertisers tell us that if we buy the right products we can avoid not only suffering but also the smallest inconveniences. A popular commercial for pain relief used to tell us that when we hurt, even a little bit, time counts—not hours of time but mere seconds!

However, Jesus and his gospel teach us that suffering is a natural part of human life; indeed, it is essential for the Christian life. As Christians, we are invited to accompany Jesus on his journey, and we cannot avoid suffering if we do so. There may seem to be a tension in the Gospels between Jesus' raising someone from the dead and himself setting out resolutely toward Jerusalem and the Cross that awaits him on Calvary. But as Cardinal Bernardin shows us, if we walk with Jesus and listen attentively to his words, we will begin to understand how this tension is resolved—how his suffering and death leads to new life. We will join him on the journey to peace.

FAITH MEANS SAYING YES TO GOD'S CALL AND PROMISES

The LORD said to Abram: "Go forth from
the land of your kinsfolk and from your father's
house to a land that I will show you.
"I will make of you a great nation,
and I will bless you;
I will make your name great,
so that you will be a blessing.
I will bless those who bless you
and curse those who curse you.
All the communities of the earth
shall find blessing in you."
Abram went as the LORD directed.

(GENESIS 12:1–4a)

Once upon a time there lived an elderly husband and
wife, named Abraham and Sarah. . . . They were sev-
enty-five years old and were slowing down noticeably.
They grew tired more easily and spent more time sitting
and reminiscing about the past. They had had a fairly
good, normal life. They had worked hard and enjoyed
the company of their family and friends. They also had
one regret: They had never been able to have children.

Despite their barrenness, they lived a settled, secure life. But they had nothing more to look forward to.

Then, one day, God entered their lives in an extraordinary way. He asked them to go on a journey that would take them far away from their home, their family, and their friends, and lead them toward a dangerously open-ended destination. God promised them well-being, prosperity, and a family of their own—but at the risk of leaving behind everything that they held dear, everything they counted on. God's wonderful promises of blessing, land, and a family were dependent on the stark requirement that Abraham and Sarah relinquish, renounce, and abandon their settled, secure lifestyle. Their future, if they chose to accept it, would be entirely dependent on God's promises. The stakes were very high! The risks were enormous! Who in their right minds would agree to take such a gamble—especially at such an advanced age? Only people of deep faith—like Abraham and Sarah.

When they left Haran in response to God's call and promises, they were, in effect, leaving behind a community that had long ago stopped listening to God—a community, therefore, that had ceased to hope—a cold, barren community with no foreseeable future. God called Abraham and Sarah to a different kind of community—one that truly listened to God's word and, therefore, enjoyed new life and hope for the future. But this came at the great human cost of entrusting their lives fully to nothing more—and nothing less—than God's promises, holding nothing of themselves back.

Today, the journey of faith remains a venture of great risks and costs. Ultimately, it requires us to renounce reliance on any and every human resource in order to acknowledge our utter dependence on God for everything. This does not come easily to us. We are used to relying on others and, especially, on ourselves. That is why it is very important that we come together regularly . . . to stand in God's presence, sing his praises, open our minds and hearts to listen to his word, and acknowledge our need for his help so that we might walk in *his* ways, not in those of the world.

As a Christian community of faith, we know the rest of the story of God's promises that eventually overcame the barrenness of Abraham and Sarah and brought blessing to all the nations of the earth. Despite their advanced age, Sarah conceived and bore a son, Isaac, the father of Jacob. And from this family line came God's chosen people, Israel. Eventually, the people of Israel settled in the Promised Land. And from this stock was born Jesus, the long-awaited Messiah, the one through whom all peoples and nations receive God's blessing.

Like Abraham and Sarah, you and I have been invited to be a community that truly listens to God's word and relies on his promises. We are called to embark on a journey of faith whose route and destination only God knows. (March 7, 1993)

Loving, almighty God, help me to recognize that my life is ultimately in your hands and to align my attitudes and actions with my faith. Help me to listen attentively to your call and give me the courage to undertake the next segment of my journey in faith despite its risks and dangers. Stay close to me!

EVERY FOLLOWER OF CHRIST MUST CHOOSE THE PATH TO TAKE

He began to teach them that the Son of Man had to suffer much, be rejected by the elders, the chief priests, and the scribes, be put to death, and rise three days later. He said these things quite openly. Peter then took him aside and began to remonstrate with him. At this he turned around and, eyeing the disciples, reprimanded Peter: "Get out of my sight, you satan! You are not judging by God's standards but by man's!"

He summoned the crowd with his disciples and

said to them: "If a man wishes to come after me, he
must deny his very self, take up his cross, and follow in my steps. Whoever would preserve his life
will lose it, but whoever loses his life for my sake
and the gospel's will preserve it."

(MARK 8:31–35)

Anyone who has ever spent a night in the hospital knows
the sounds of suffering. Anyone who has ever walked in
the city's housing projects after dark, or a nursing home
by day, or spent even an hour in a prison, knows the
sounds of anger, the sounds of fear, the sounds of despair—all of the complex harmonies of suffering.

And they are terrible sounds. They may echo and
re-echo within us like a bad dream until we feel com-
pelled to muffle them under the more normal, pleasant
sounds of our daily routines. But for most of us, they
are sounds that silence simply cannot erase.

He began to teach them that the Son of Man had to
suffer much . . . that the Son of Man had much to
suffer.

(MARK 8:31)

It is a normal, instinctive response to run from suffering. We try to avoid it for ourselves, and we make every

effort to protect our loved ones from it. Suffering is perceived as a dire threat to our life and happiness.

Our dread of suffering is so strong that we not only seek to shelter ourselves from it, but sometimes we shun others who suffer, even our friends and family, in our effort to escape its pleading voices.

Those who have been divorced sometimes report that their friends and family no longer invite them to parties. At times, those who have been fired or laid off tell us that when they encounter their former colleagues, they are met with embarrassed silence.

Cancer patients and others who suffer with serious illness notice that their former friends have difficulty looking at them, eye to eye. We don't know what to say. The pitch and volume of suffering reduces us to silence.

Jesus tells us, however, that in that silence *life* begins! "Whoever would preserve his life will lose it, but whoever loses his life for my sake and the gospel's will preserve it" (Mark 8:35).

VERONICA HAS BEEN A WIDOW for many, many years. She has three grown children. After her husband died, she had to go to work to support her young family. So her parents came to live with her to help her raise her children and keep her house. That was some forty years ago.

Veronica's aged mother is in a nursing home now. Several years ago she fell and broke her hip. Veronica visits her every day and spends most of the day at the nursing home. She and her mother listen to the ball game or work crossword puzzles together. Sometimes they just sit holding hands. One doesn't have to ask her why she does it, but sometimes Veronica will say, "All my life I have tried to do my duty. In my life, duty was the shape my love took."

For Jesus' followers, love—by God's standards—is measured not by the peace and happiness it brings to the one who loves; rather, by the peace and happiness it brings to the one who *is* loved. And, of course, the paradox of Christian love is that it doubles back—"good measure pressed down, shaken together, running over" (Luke 6:38).

"Whoever loses his life for my sake and the gospel's will preserve it."

(MARK 8:35b)

For every follower of Christ there comes a choice, when the path veers off toward the Cross. The wisdom of the world raises an alarm: Turn back, beware, ahead lies your destruction! But in our hearts a softer, firmer voice invites us, "Come, follow me, and I will show you the path of life." (September 15, 1991)

Lord God, creator of all life, give me the wisdom and the courage to face and, indeed, embrace suffering whenever I encounter it. Help me to follow your Son Jesus along the path that leads to everlasting life.

JESUS WANTS TO BE THE LORD OF OUR LIVES

Soon afterward he went to a town called Naim, and his disciples and a large crowd accompanied him. As he approached the gate of the town a dead man was being carried out, the only son of a widowed mother. A considerable crowd of townsfolk were with her. The Lord was moved with pity upon seeing her and said to her, "Do not cry." Then he stepped forward and touched the litter; at this, the bearers halted. He said, "Young man, I bid you get up." The dead man sat up and began to speak. Then Jesus gave him back to his mother. Fear seized them all and they began to praise God.

"A great prophet has risen among us," they said;
and, "God has visited his people." This was the report that spread about him throughout Judea and
the surrounding country.

(LUKE 7:11–17)

What brings us together . . . during every celebration of
the Eucharist is the story of *Jesus*. As we know, no sin-
gle story does justice to the full meaning of his life, mission, and ministry. And so each week—and every
day—we listen and reflect on the Gospel so that we
might acquire a better appreciation of all God has revealed to us—and done for us—in Jesus.

Jesus' concern for the widow of Naim is a touching,
familiar story. In this simple narrative we discover several things about Jesus.

First, he is very *sensitive* to human hurt and suffering. Jesus is not like those who pass by someone in
need, looking the other way. He is very attentive to the
tears of the widow of Naim, just as he is to those who
approach him with a request for healing.

He is also *compassionate*. When he encounters the
funeral procession and learns that the woman is a
widow who has lost her only son, he is "moved with
pity upon seeing her" (Luke 7:13a). Throughout the

Gospels we witness Jesus' compassion—toward the sick and the suffering, toward the poor, toward the crowds that mill about like sheep without a shepherd.

In his healing touch, we learn that Jesus is *all-powerful*. Like the prophets of old—Elijah and Elisha—he is able to bring the young man back to life and give him back to his mother. The miraculous act stuns the crowd, who acclaim him a great prophet, but—interestingly enough—are not yet ready to declare him Lord of their lives.

In this brief, beautiful story we get a wonderful glimpse of what God is truly like—sensitive to our needs and compassionate toward suffering—all-powerful and loving.

The same risen Lord continues to be present in our midst. We continue to experience and share his love, which also makes many demands on us. Indeed, Jesus' love can at times be "tough love" because it calls us to live a life that is in accord with the values he taught us—values that often stand in opposition to the values of our contemporary society and its culture.

In fact, the real meaning of [the Christian] community—at its deepest level—is to be found in the way *we live our lives* as his disciples. For he is the Lord of our lives, our hearts. (June 11, 1989)

*O God, our Creator and Redeemer, help me to be-
come a true disciple of the risen Lord. Help me to
be more like him: sensitive, compassionate and loving. Open my mind, my heart, my entire being so
that he will truly be the Lord of my life.*

YET, TRUE DISCIPLESHIP IS NEVER EASY

He went through cities and towns teaching—all
the while making his way toward Jerusalem.
Someone asked him, "Lord, are they few in number who are to be saved?" He replied: "Try to
come in through the narrow door. Many, I tell
you, will try to enter and be unable. When once
the master of the house has risen to lock the door
and you stand outside knocking and saying, 'Sir,
open for us,' he will say in reply, 'I do not know
where you come from.' Then you will begin to
say, 'We ate and drank in your company. You
taught in our streets.' But he will answer, 'I tell
you, I do not know where you come from. Away
from me, you evildoers!'

"There will be wailing and grinding of teeth
when you see Abraham, Isaac, Jacob, and all the

prophets safe in the kingdom of God, and you yourselves rejected. People will come from the east and the west, from the north and the south, and will take their place at the feast in the kingdom of God. Some who are last will be first and some who are first will be last."

(LUKE 13:22–30)

It is not easy to be a true disciple of Jesus. It involves considerable cost and risk. . . .

The gospel reminds us, first of all, that Jesus is on his way to Jerusalem. There he will give up his life on Calvary to save the human family and be raised up in glory. It is no simple matter to lay down one's life for friends—let alone for sinners! But Jesus, who came among us "filled with enduring love" (John 1:14d), was willing to make that supreme sacrifice. Such is God's great love for us!

The man who asks Jesus whether many will be saved (Luke 13:23) is curious about *others*. Jesus redirects the question to express concern about the man *himself*. Not everyone who "seeks" will "enter" God's kingdom, Jesus says. Then he adds that his disciples—including us—should "try to come in through the narrow door" (Luke 13:24).

In other words, despite the fact that God loves us

fully and eternally, this, of itself, does not *guarantee* each of us a place in his kingdom. Rather, we must *live* in accord with the vision and values of the gospel. We must put our beliefs into practice. We must carry out God's will and observe his law. God does not impose his love on us. He expects us freely to receive his love into our lives and to respond with love—by ridding our lives of sin and selfishness, and by learning how to love him and one another.

Jesus observes that some people live under the sad illusion that they are following him, but, in fact, their relationship with him is very casual (Luke 13:26–27). Some eat and drink at table with him but never enter into a truly intimate relationship with him. Some hear his teaching but do not accept it as God's word that is to be put into practice, so it can shape their lives.

Many want to have a special place at the messianic banquet, but some—perhaps many—will be sorely disappointed to discover that those they consider outcasts or "outsiders" will have a place at God's table while they themselves will be turned away (Luke 13:28–29).

If we want to enter into God's kingdom, we must fully commit our lives to the risen Lord—holding nothing back from him. This is what it means to enter "the narrow door."

Jesus invites us to walk with him toward Jerusalem.

The letter to the Hebrews says that this will take much discipline on our part. It urges us to "strengthen [our] drooping hands and [our] weak knees" and to "make straight the paths [we] walk on" (Hebrews 12:12–13). There are trials to be endured on the journey to the kingdom; they are the price of justice and peace. There are paths to be straightened, even as we walk on them. There is healing to be brought to those who find the journey too difficult or threatening to undertake alone.

Walking with Jesus captures what it means to be a Christian and a Catholic community of faith. (August 23, 1992)

O God, source of all goodness and blessing, thank you for the gift of your beloved Son. Lead me to conversion, to a change of mind, heart and spirit so that I will have the courage to walk with him, even to Calvary and the Cross.

The invitation to a journey has been made. Not just any journey, but the one at the heart of Christian life. The one that leads to Calvary. The one that leads to salvation, new life and peace.

Are you willing to accept it?

If so, stop a moment and just be. Find a quiet place without distractions. Relax. Take a few deep breaths, breathing out tension and anxiety and breathing in peace and serenity.

Now, prayerfully place yourself in the hands of the Lord. Trust in God's love and fidelity. Let go.

Unlike as in so much of your daily life, you are not now in a race to reach the end. Take your time. This book is meant to be read in small portions throughout the year.

With Joseph Bernardin as your guide, read the text, imagine yourself at the particular Station and ask what it means for your life. If it helps, record your feelings and insights in a journal, share them with a trusted friend, meditate more deeply on them with a spiritual director.

Each time you read and reflect on the Stations, you will discover new things about who God is and who you really are. Each step of the Way of the Cross is a step closer to peace and freedom. As disciples, we are called to walk the journey of faith, hope and love so that we can work together in transforming the world into the kingdom of God. Let us begin our journey with the confidence to face all that we encounter and the assurance of things hoped for but not yet seen.

O God, the source of all life and goodness, help us to prepare for the next stage of our journey. Help us to leave behind the stress and tension of each day so that we can sit serenely in your presence even as we accompany your Son through his Passion, death and resurrection. Send your Holy Spirit into our lives so that we may gain wisdom, understanding and peace. And help us to share our gifts with all our brothers and sisters.

First Station

JESUS IS CONDEMNED
TO DEATH

To be condemned for a serious crime that one has committed is a terrifying moment in one's life. To be condemned for a crime that one has not committed—to be condemned when one is innocent—is both a grave injustice and a personally humiliating moment.

In the Old Testament, prophets who proclaimed God's word to his people often experienced opposition, ridicule, condemnation and even death. Jesus knew his Jewish tradition well and understood that his mission and message would be opposed by some, even the majority of his listeners. But he remained faithful to his mission and assented to his Father's will.

Throughout his life, Cardinal Bernardin also paid the price many times for remaining faithful to his pastoral mission. An influential figure, Bernardin spoke out publicly against nuclear weapons, abortion, euthanasia. He called for a consistent ethic of life and for common-ground dialogue. At times he met opposition and made enemies. He also knew the sting of false accusation. But he accepted these hardships as the necessary price of being a believer, and he encouraged us to do the same.

The First Station of the Cross stands in sharp contrast with Jesus' triumphal entry into Jerusalem only a few days earlier. Then some of his disciples, caught up in the excitement of the event, had loudly proclaimed,

"Blessed is he who comes as king
in the name of the Lord!"
(Luke 19:38).
Now Jesus stands alone; his disciples have scattered. And the
crowd calls for the death penalty: "Crucify him!"

Pilate addressed them again, for he wanted Jesus to be the one released.

But they shouted back, "Crucify him, crucify him!" He said to them for the third time, "What wrong is this man guilty of? I have not discovered anything about him that calls for the death penalty. I will therefore chastise him and release him." But they demanded with loud cries that he be crucified, and their shouts increased in violence. Pilate then decreed that what they demanded should be done. He released the one they asked for, who had been thrown in prison for insurrection and murder, and delivered Jesus up to their wishes.

(LUKE 23:20–25)

JESUS ACCEPTED THE PRICE OF
BEING A PROPHET

The Gospels often portray Jesus as an itinerant prophet who is led by God's Spirit. Like the lives of the prophets of old, Jesus' life is not his own. It belongs entirely to his Father who sent him into the world with a prophetic, saving, reconciling mission. Prophetic ministry is often difficult because the prophet's message falls on deaf ears, is unpopular or countercultural, or is resisted with outright hostility. Moreover, people sometimes—wittingly or unwittingly—try to lure a prophet from his God-given mission. . . .

Jesus often confronted serious obstacles to his mission. Let's focus our attention on this dimension of his prophetic ministry. If we are truly united with the Lord, we will experience both his joys and sorrows, his peaceful moments as well as the tense ones. I am particularly impressed with the way Jesus responded to pressures, hostility, intrigue, fickleness, shallowness, indifference. Despite the fact that he is God's Son, Jesus had to grapple with the diverse forces of his day—just as we do. That is why—if we want to understand ourselves and our own ministry better—we must first focus on Jesus and learn from his ministry.

At various times and in diverse ways, Jesus faced the fierce hostility of both *demons* and *humans.* As we know from the events during the last week of his public ministry, a very fine line divided the crowd chanting "hosannas" from those demanding his death. Particularly intense was the hostility of those whose very task and purpose in life were challenged by his message. At times only Jesus' moral authority was challenged. At other times, however, his very life was threatened!

Grappling with difficult issues and people each day is part and parcel of our ministry. We cannot reasonably expect to escape from it. Why? Because the message we proclaim often goes against the grain; it is not what some people want to hear. In many instances it goes against the mores of the moment. But it helps us to know that this was very much a part of Jesus' own life and ministry—that he, too, had to deal with it each day. He was able—but not without considerable cost to himself—to confront successfully the hostility of the crowds and demons as he went about proclaiming the Good News. (May 16, 1990)

> *O God, my strength and my shield, give me the integrity and the courage to proclaim the risen Lord and his gospel faithfully. Help me acquire the per-*

spective of faith when I encounter opposition to
your word, so that I may be united with your Son in
his humiliation and suffering for your greater glory.

THE BURDEN OF THE CROSS IS HEAVY INDEED

Allow me to share with you some of what I have
learned about the truth of this during the past three and
a half months. On Thursday, November 11, [1993], the
media carried the story that I was going to be sued in a
sexual misconduct case. I had heard rumors of such a
suit earlier in the day but did not know what the specific
allegation entailed. You can imagine how I felt! The
next morning, Friday, as I was reciting the Rosary as
part of my morning prayer, I began to meditate on the
sorrowful mysteries. When I began with the "agony in
the garden," I was suddenly able to understand much
more deeply than ever before what that moment meant
in Jesus' life. I felt very close to him in his agony, and
also asked the Father, "Why me?"

The past three and a half months have been very
painful. I was very embarrassed by the charges, which
I knew were absolutely false. I had to stand—literally
before the entire world—again and again to declare my
innocence. Fortunately, I received a great outpouring of
support from throughout the Archdiocese and, indeed,

the entire country and the world. But I was also very disturbed by those who seemed, on the mere basis of the widely publicized charge, to assume that I was guilty.

The love and prayers of so many friends were a great comfort to me. But I would not have survived the burden of this cross had it not been for the time I spent in prayer each day. Ultimately, it was only my intimacy with the Lord—which grew and deepened these past few months—that enabled me to have a sense of inner peace, which in turn allowed me to continue my pastoral ministry each day. As I said earlier, this is a great mystery, but our suffering can bring us very close to Jesus. And that makes all the difference in the world! (March 6, 1994)

My God, your beloved Son encountered the mystery
of suffering throughout his life, but, when he stood
before Pilate, he entered into that mystery more
deeply. Help me to accept suffering in my life by
uniting myself more closely with the risen Lord
through prayer each day.

WITH GOD'S LOVE WE LACK NOTHING

The question "Why me?" has been asked by countless people through the ages. That question crossed *my* mind, I assure you. As you know, [in November 1993] I had suffered the humiliation of a false accusation of sexual misconduct. So when I discovered that I had cancer [in June 1995], I wondered why God had also allowed this to happen to me. We often tend to assume for some reason that when hardship or tragedies occur, God has punished or abandoned us. But in his letter to the Romans, Saint Paul lays that assumption to rest once and for all. No creature—absolutely no one—can separate us from God's all-powerful love that comes to us through his Son, Jesus (Romans 8:38–39). No adversity can prevent our access to God's love. God has *not* rejected or abandoned us. His love for us is absolute, not conditional. And if we have God's love, we have all we need. We lack nothing. (September 14, 1996)

Loving God, I, too, sometimes ask myself—and you—why something bad has happened to me. Deepen my faith and trust in you so that I will truly believe that nothing can separate me from your love. With the assurance of your love, I will lack nothing!

JESUS BEARS HIS CROSS

When Cardinal Bernardin made a pastoral visit to Lithuania in August 1990, he was well aware of the great suffering, the cross that Catholics there had borne for decades under Communism. They had remained steadfastly loyal in their faith, looking forward to a time in the future when they would experience resurrection and new life. Because of Jesus' death and resurrection, the forces of evil have been definitively conquered, even though the struggle continues in our own lives and times.

Most of us have not faced a similar, decades-long period of darkness as have those who lived in countries under Communist rule. At the same time, there are many kinds of crosses, and we cannot entirely escape from bearing them. Many of us would naturally prefer to celebrate the joy of Easter without having to undergo the pain of Good Friday. Peter is not alone in his resistance to hearing Jesus' predictions of his Passion, death and resurrection. But Jesus' example of bearing his Cross in this Second Station inspires us to look more deeply into the mystery of redemptive suffering. It will also help us accept alienation from others and even from God—a special kind of cross.

Finally, when they had finished making a fool of him, they stripped him of the cloak, dressed him in his own clothes, and led him off to crucifixion.

(MATTHEW 27:31)

SUFFERING AND THE CROSS ARE AT
THE HEART OF CHRISTIANITY

Suffering and the Cross are at the very heart of the Christian faith. In his letter to the Corinthians (1 Corinthians 1:22–25), Saint Paul tells us about the paradox of the Cross. Suffering and death are signs of human weakness, defeat. It is for many an obstacle, a scandal, a stumbling block. But Jesus turned suffering and death into victory.

If we are to share in that victory, we, too, must be willing to take up *our* cross and follow him. There are, of course, many costs and risks involved in being his disciple. . . . But we know that the Cross is always followed by the resurrection—sometimes after a long period of suffering, persecution, and even martyrdom. (August 31, 1990)

God, my refuge and my strength, help me to accept, even embrace, the crosses that I encounter in my life. Teach me what it means to be an authentic disciple of your beloved Son. Transform my human weakness into steadfastness.

FOLLOWING CHRIST MEANS
BEARING OUR CROSSES

When Jesus invites us to follow him, the Cross is embossed at the very center of the invitation. For most of us, this is not a call to martyrdom. Rather, Jesus asks for our steadfast loyalty to him and his way of life each day. We are not to be ashamed of or abandon our commitment to him and his gospel.

He does not ask something of us that he himself was unwilling to do. Saint Paul writes that, in responding to his Father's will, Jesus "was not alternately 'yes' and 'no'; he was never anything but 'yes' " (2 Corinthians 1:19). Obedience to the Father's will is at the heart of evangelical obedience. . . . In the Garden of Gethsemane, Jesus prays, "Father, if it is your will, take this cup from me; yet not my will but yours be done" (Luke 22:42). (May 17, 1990)

Lord, God of hosts, help me to walk in your ways, saying yes to you in my everyday life, even when what you ask of me seems more than I can humanly bear. Walk with me and help me to persevere.

In Matthew's Gospel (17:1–8), we encounter Jesus transfigured on a mountain, with Moses and Elijah at his side. We stand with the three disciples—Peter, James, and John—and witness an event filled with great mystery. What can this mean? Who is this Jesus?

Peter is apparently overcome with awe and offers to build booths or tents for Jesus, Moses, and Elijah. What does Peter have in mind? Perhaps he simply wants to prolong this awesome moment as long as possible. Perhaps he prefers to stay on the mountain rather than continue the journey to Jerusalem, where, as Jesus had predicted, a painful death awaited the Lord. Perhaps Peter simply doesn't know what to say and says the first thing that comes to his mind. It wouldn't be the first time he spoke or acted impulsively!

At any rate, Peter does not understand the vision on his own. His voice is silenced by a voice from heaven. Speaking from a bright cloud, God the Father repeats what he said at Jesus' baptism: "This is my beloved Son on whom my favor rests. *Listen to him*!" (Matthew 17:5) [emphasis added]. That helps explain what is happening. Just before Jesus took the three disciples up the mountain where he was to be transfigured, Peter had professed that Jesus was the Messiah, "the Son of the living God" (Matthew 16:16). Then Jesus had explained that they were on their way to Jerusalem, where he would suffer, die, and rise again. Peter had immediately protested. This was not *his* idea of a Messiah! Jesus sharply rebuked him for judging by the world's standards, not by God's.

Now, on the mountain of the transfiguration, Peter hears directly from God the Father that he and the other disciples are to listen carefully to everything Jesus tells them. His instruction about how to live a good, moral life is intimately connected with his understanding of the necessity of suffering. To walk in his way involves costs and risks. Following in Jesus' footsteps often entails suffering because it is not the way of the world, and his followers often suffer ridicule and opposition. But loving one's enemies despite ill treatment and persecution—in imitation of Jesus—is a creative use of suffering in obedience to God's will.

The three disciples come down from the mountain with Jesus, and their lives are changed forever. Nothing can ever be the same again. They have gotten a glimpse of Jesus' heavenly glory. But one more experience awaits them near Jerusalem. He will invite them to join him in the Garden of Gethsemane, where they will also witness his human glory as he wrestles with God's will for himself. All disciples who wish to share Jesus' future glory must also be willing to share in his suffering. There is no other way. This is a sobering thought, but one that is more than balanced by God's promises of salvation, hope, and everlasting life.

Like Peter, James, and John, we ask God's help to see persons and events in the light of faith, and to have the courage and strength to follow Jesus—even to Calvary. My prayer for you . . . is that God will deepen your faith, hope, and love so that you might be faithful witnesses of his promises wherever your pilgrim way takes you. (March 7, 1993)

Lord God, there is so much noise in my world, in my life, that makes it difficult to hear my own inner thoughts, let alone listen to the words of your beloved Son. Help me to acquire the kind of inner peace that will open my being to your word so that I can respond appropriately.

ACCEPTING ALIENATION AS A FORM OF EMBRACING THE CROSS

We sometimes experience alienation in our relationships with *others*. This is what usually comes to mind when we think of alienation. It's not difficult to make a list of people we don't get along with, persons with whom we often disagree, individuals we simply don't like. The alienation may stem from a hurtful experience or even a series of them. While we may be able to be reconciled with some people, others may keep us at a distance and refuse us entry into a more intimate encounter where reconciliation can take place. Of course, we can do the same to others as well . . .

The racial or ethnic background of people, their cultural heritage, their personal values and beliefs may be quite different from our own. We or they may be set in our ways, and it may seem impossible, humanly speaking, to bridge the chasm between them and us. So, alienation—at times, a very painful experience—perdures.

We should not be surprised if we sometimes experience alienation from *God*. As we know, sin can rupture our relationship with God. However, even when we pray regularly, God may, at times, seem more absent than present. Even Saint Teresa of Ávila experienced a dark night of the soul.

Accepting the fact of alienation is the equivalent of embracing the Cross each day, approaching suffering as Jesus himself did. (May 15, 1990)

God of glory and majesty, I acknowledge that you are the Lord of my life. Without you I can do nothing. But please do not hide your face from me. And if that is what I do experience, allow me to approach this suffering, too, as Jesus himself did.

JESUS FALLS FOR THE FIRST TIME

When people think of a "fall," they often think of a "fall from grace." However, this first fall of Jesus on the way to Calvary is caused by the sheer weight of the Cross and the toll of Jesus' suffering. It is embarrassing to fall, even when the cause is clear or it has been brought about by others. Falling is a sign of weakness, and it can be very humiliating.

What is important is the ability to get back up and continue the journey. Cardinal Bernardin was able to do this when he "fell"—for example, when he was falsely accused of sexual misconduct, when he was diagnosed as having cancer and later when he learned that it was terminal. These kinds of falls brought the cardinal closer to the suffering and crucified Christ and to all those to whom he ministered. Our falls can do the same for us. But our falls, our suffering put us to the test: Is our faith strong enough to act out and live on? Through our faith and God's help, can we rise out of the darkness and live in the light of the Lord?

Have pity on me, O God, for men trample
      upon me;
   all the day they press this attack against me . . .
O Most High, when I begin to fear,
   in you will I trust.

(PSALM 56:2, 3)

FAITH IS A GREAT GIFT TO BE LIVED

Saint Paul . . . reminds us that faith is a great gift, a gift to be treasured but not a gift to be put away. It is rather a gift that is to be lived, to be put into practice, if it is to be alive and effective. This is the challenge we all face: How do we deepen our own faith so that we can put it into practice? How do we live as examples of faith to others? How do we best hear and respond to the call of God in our lives?

Jesus . . . extends the call to each of us to follow him and hopes that we will respond. But he reminds us that it will not always be easy. At times we will feel that we are literally carrying a cross—that we are experiencing much of the same pain that Jesus did in his own life. But somehow we know that it is all worth it. The hope that Jesus offers not only strengthens our conviction but also deepens the faith we receive as a gift. (September 11, 1994)

Almighty God, sometimes my burdens are too heavy
for me. They bring me to my knees. While this may
be interpreted as a sign of weakness, it also deepens
the faith that you have given me. Thank you for
teaching me, even in my weakest moments.

I was very humiliated. It was total humiliation. Last Friday morning, as I always do, early in the morning I was praying my Rosary, and on Fridays we use the sorrowful mysteries. The first mystery, as you so well know, is the Agony in the Garden. And as I prayed that decade of the Rosary, I said to the Lord, "In all my sixty-five years, this is the first time that I have really understood the pain and the agony you felt that night." And then I said, "Why did you let it happen?" I never felt more alone.

Last Friday afternoon, just a week ago, at 1:00 P.M., I had to stand before the world and did feel very much alone. Up to that point I had felt supported, but when I went into the conference room on the first floor of the Pastoral Center and saw some sixty or seventy media representatives, I did feel very much alone. And the only thing I had going for me at that moment was my own forty-two years of ordained ministry, my name, my reputation. But there was an inner strength. And I am convinced that that inner strength was the strength the Lord had given me.

For me, it was a moment of grace. A moment of pain, but also a moment of grace, because after that I began receiving the kind of support, the expressions of

love, that I did not think were possible. But it was also
a moment of grace because, for me personally, it was a
time of spiritual growth. I have talked to many of you
about my own spiritual journey, but I can assure you
that I am entering into a new phase of that journey because of all that has happened during the past week.
(November 19, 1993)

God of compassion and mercy, help me to see your
grace at work even in moments of pain. I know that
it is not easy, but with your assistance I believe that
pain and suffering will deepen me spiritually and
draw me closer to you.

DO NOT DESPAIR, FOR GOD
IS ALWAYS WITH US

When we are ill or no longer able to function as we
used to, it is not only the physical pain or incapacity that
affects us. Our mind and our heart, our imagination and
our will are also affected. In 1987, on a pastoral visit to
New Zealand, Pope John Paul II celebrated a communal
Anointing of the Sick. . . . He told the people, "when
pain dulls the mind and weighs down body and soul,

God can seem far away; life can become a heavy burden. We are tempted not to believe the Good News." We "may even be led to the verge of despair."

The Anointing of the Sick reminds us of God's plan for our salvation: how God allowed his own beloved Son to suffer, die, and rise again so that we might be saved, so that we might be forever convinced of his enduring, unconditional love for each of us! The death and resurrection of Jesus—the paschal mystery—is the triumph of life over death. (September 14, 1996)

> *God, the source of all life, thank you for the precious gift of life. Help me to become free by not clinging too tightly to my life. When the burdens of life become heavy and cause me to fall, help me to get back up—even when the end of my life is near.*

OUR SUFFERING BRINGS US CLOSER TO JESUS

The U.S. pollster George Gallup has conducted several surveys on religion in America in recent years. He reports that the vast majority of Americans consistently identify themselves as believers. That appears to be good news! But Gallup probes a bit deeper in his questions and has discovered some disturbing trends in many persons' concept of religion.

While many say they believe in God, it is only belief in an affirming, loving God—*not* one who makes demands on us. They pray, but the emphasis is on asking for things for themselves—*not* on praising God, thanking him for his blessings, or asking his forgiveness for their sins. In other words, some believers want all the benefits and fruits of faith but none of its responsibilities or obligations.

That kind of "easy street" brand of religion is *not* what we encounter in Scripture. [For example, Exodus 20:1–17] is a solemn proclamation of the Ten Commandments—the way of life demanded from those who belong to God's chosen people. The commandments tell us both what *not* to do—do not kill, do not steal—and what we *are* to do—keep holy the Sabbath, honor your father and your mother.

If we are honest with ourselves, these are not unreasonable demands. They protect the community from harmful, disruptive behavior. They help each of us to live in a right relationship with everyone else so that we can enjoy the fruits of justice, harmony, and peace. Moreover, the commandments are not really that difficult to observe, if we but make the effort—and help one another. It has been shown over and over again that when parents live by the Ten Commandments, their children are also much more likely to do so—and their grandchildren as well.

Nevertheless, living the Catholic religion goes deeper than observing the Ten Commandments. And this is where faith becomes more difficult. The Church's fundamental mission is to proclaim the Lord Jesus and his gospel. And the Jesus we preach is Christ *crucified*, as Saint Paul points out [1 Corinthians 1:22–25]. This reminds us of something very important: *It is impossible to embrace Jesus without embracing the cross as well.*

In an earlier verse in that same letter to the Corinthians, Saint Paul reminds them—and us—that "the message of the cross is complete absurdity to those who are headed for ruin, but to us who are experiencing salvation it is the power of God" (1 Corinthians 1:18).

[John] also points to the Cross (2:13–25). In the dramatic episode of the cleansing of the Temple in Jerusalem, Jesus tells his critics that although they may put him to death, he will rise again on the third day. And that is important for us to hear. The Cross is not the end of the road! It is one significant moment on a pilgrimage that leads to resurrection and new life!

Saint Paul also tells us that the Cross reveals God's

wisdom and power. His power is a *saving* power, and his wisdom is a *life-giving* wisdom. This means that the Cross plays a special role in our own lives when we join our sufferings to those of Christ. Jesus has opened his suffering to each of us and has also shared the suffering of all of us. He invites us to pick up our cross daily as we follow him. He calls us to unite ourselves with him in our suffering. This is the great mystery, but the truth is that our suffering can bring us very close to Jesus. (March 6, 1994)

> *Loving God, I have learned that it is not easy to walk in faith with your Son Jesus. Yes, I look forward to the resurrection and new life, but, humanly speaking, I would prefer to escape the Cross, today or any day of my life. Help me, instead, to embrace the Cross!*

LIVE IN GOD'S LIGHT

If you accept the Lord's peace into your hearts, the darkness will not be able to overwhelm you. There is nothing that you and God cannot face together. God's love revealed in Jesus is the most powerful force the universe will ever know. All the heartbreak, misery, and suffering cannot overcome his love. Reach for it! Accept it into your heart!

Do not make a home for yourself in the darkness. You have been created for the light of God's love! God's greatest desire is for you to live in his light, to know his love, to experience his peace. I urge you to open your minds and hearts to receive that gift today! (Feast of the Holy Family, 1986)

God of light, there is so much darkness in our world and in my life at times. Pull me out of the darkness into your own wonderful light. Whatever my circumstances, allow me to stand in the circle of your light and love—and share it with others.

JESUS MEETS HIS MOTHER

When we think of Jesus meeting his mother along the way to Calvary, it is easy to think of a mother's heart "pierced with a sword," as predicted by Simeon when Jesus was first presented as a child in the Temple at Jerusalem (cf. Luke 2:22–35). But there is more than first meets the eye in this Fourth Station. In the Gospels, Mary is a woman of strength and courage. Unlike Eve in the Garden of Eden, Mary says yes to God not only at the Incarnation but also throughout her life. Truly, she is the first Christian disciple because of her faith and trust in God. And therefore she is a model for each of us on our pilgrim way.

Joseph Bernardin shared a deep love for his own mother, Maria, with a profound devotion to Mary, the Mother of God. When at six years old he lost his father to cancer, his mother's strong faith nourished Joseph and his younger sister, Elaine, and held the family together. Bernardin learned well early on about the power of faith, and two of his most important models were Maria and Mary.

In 1984, at a very difficult time in the history of Poland, Cardinal Bernardin reminded Catholics at Częstochowa on Mary's feast of how Mary found freedom in the truth even when the truth involved suffering. This Fourth Station calls us all to do the same.

Simeon blessed them and said to Mary his mother:
"This child is destined to be the downfall and the

rise of many in Israel, a sign that will be
opposed—and you yourself shall be pierced
with a sword—so that the thoughts of many
hearts may be laid bare."

(LUKE 2:34-35)

MARY IS A WOMAN OF STRENGTH
AND COURAGE

One cannot really understand our Christian faith unless
one accepts and appreciates the Incarnation. The pivotal
point of our faith is the fact that God redeemed us by
becoming one of us. God's Son, Jesus, took his flesh
from the Virgin Mary, and he redeemed us through his
humanity: It was through his Passion, death, and resurrection that he reconciled us with his Father. As Paul
told the Galatians, "When the designated time had
come, God sent forth his Son born of a woman, born
under the law, to deliver from the law those who were
subjected to it, so that we might receive our status as
adopted [children] . . ." (Galatians 4: 4–5). . . .

THE LATE POPE PAUL VI published a beautiful apostolic letter on Mary and Marian devotion in 1975. In that letter he said that Mary is a model for us today, not because of the precise type of life she led or the social and cultural environment in which she lived (since this hardly exists anymore), but because in her own personal life she fully and responsibly accepted the will of God. She heard the Word of God and was obedient to it. When God revealed to her, through the angel Gabriel, that she was to be the mother of his Son, she did not and could not understand all the implications. Her first response was an indication of how perplexed she was: "How can this be since I do not know man?" (Luke 1:34). She was bewildered, even terrified. And yet she said without any hesitation, "I am the servant of the Lord. Let it be done to me as you say" (Luke 1:38).

The Holy Father also suggested another reason Mary can be an example for the rest of us. He admitted that some of the past images of Mary are so removed from real life that it is understandable that some people will think it too unreasonable or too idealistic to consider her an authentic model. But this is not the real Mary. The real Mary was a down-to-earth, faith-filled person who gave her active and responsible consent to the Incarnation, an event of world importance, an event—as I said earlier—that lies at the very heart of our Christian faith.

In every respect . . . Mary was a woman of strength and courage who experienced poverty and suffering, flight and exile. She was not only a mother who quite understandably was concerned with her own divine Son, but also a woman whose presence and action helped to strengthen the apostles and disciples in their faith in Christ and whose maternal role was expanded and became universal on Calvary when the dying Christ offered Mary to John and to all those who would come after him as their mother.

So we can truly say, as Pope Paul did, that Mary was a perfect Christian whose example can give us direction, strength, and inspiration as we strive to respond to the Lord's call. Indeed, it is correct to say that Mary's true greatness rests not so much in the privileges and honors that were bestowed on her in virtue of her special calling . . . as in her own intense faith, which promoted her to accept God's will joyfully and without any hesitation or reservation. (January 1, 1989)

Lord God, I thank you for the gift of Mary, the Mother of Jesus, the Mother of the Church, and the Mother of us all. Send your Holy Spirit into my life so that, like Mary, I can allow Jesus to abide within me and share him with others. By her example may I develop the strength and courage to say yes to you always.

MARY, THE FIRST DISCIPLE

Let us reflect for a few moments on Mary's wonderful song of praise [the *Magnificat*], for in that canticle Mary reveals her true greatness. In her song Mary refers to two kinds of people. On the one hand there are the *anawim:* the poor, the lowly, the sick, the downtrodden, the unfortunate. On the other hand there are the proud and the arrogant, those who feel no need of God. The lowly recognize their utter dependence on God. But the proud assert their personal power and independence from God.

Mary is first and foremost among the *anawim*. She contrasts her lowliness with God's greatness, power, holiness, and mercy. She rejoices that God is God and Mary is Mary. It is in prayer that Mary comes to know who she is—both lowly and blessed. She also comes to know who God is—the Holy One, the merciful Father, the all-powerful God, the Great One of Israel. God, Mary asserts, makes wonderful promises to his people and has both the power to realize them and the faithfulness to carry them out.

Mary is a wonderful model and a source of inspiration for *all* who seek to meet the challenges of today's Church and society. She did not run away from life and its demands. She accepted life—and her own particular role in life—freely and eagerly. She was not a timid woman. Rather . . . she proclaimed for all to hear that God vindicates the poor and the oppressed, that he dethrones the arrogant, proud, and powerful. She proclaimed a vision of God's kingdom that was *daring, challenging,* and *full of hope,* a vision that left no room for the fainthearted and complacent.

With faith and love she entrusted her entire life to God. She made an irrevocable commitment, calling herself his "handmaid." This commitment, this all-encompassing orientation, determined in a decisive way her relationship with the Lord and, indeed, with all people. Despite the suffering and hardship that were such an important part of her life, she knew the freedom and peace that come from knowing the truth and living in conformity with it. (August 15, 1996)

*God of wisdom and holiness, I admit that at times
I want to run away from life and its demands—and
sometimes do so, as you well know. Help me to
learn from Mary's example to entrust my life
entirely to you.*

MARY, OUR MODEL OF FAITH
AND TRUST IN GOD

Mary is our model of faith and trust in God, a wonderful example of how we are called to entrust our lives to the Lord. For her to be an apt model, however, she must be like us—in all things but sin. And if this is true, then Mary, too, must have found it difficult at times to be a handmaid of the Lord, to surrender her life to the Father's will. It is not always easy to see the truth about ourselves, about our relationship with God or with one another. But there is no other way to achieve freedom, no other way to bring about a transformation of our world into the kingdom of God. Mary found freedom in the truth. . . . (August 15, 1984)

Heavenly Father, it is not easy for me or any of us
to see the truth about ourselves, the world in which
we live or our relationship with you. Help me to
walk steadily along the path that leads to truth,
the truth that will set me free.

SIMON OF CYRENE HELPS JESUS CARRY HIS CROSS

*It is not difficult to imagine that Simon was somehow coerced
into helping Jesus carry his Cross. After all, he was coming
in from working in the fields and presumably was tired. Why
would he want to get involved in a procession leading to a
crucifixion?! We can identify with any reluctance on his part
because of our own hesitation to get involved in something
difficult that we may rationalize is none of our business. But
God calls us to help our neighbor, and Jesus shows us how to
do it, even when we are exhausted. Indeed, as Cardinal
Bernardin often pointed out, especially in the final months
of his life, Jesus actually helps us bear our crosses!*

> As they led him away, they laid hold of one Simon
> the Cyrenean who was coming in from the fields.
> They put a crossbeam on Simon's shoulder for him
> to carry along behind Jesus.
>
> (LUKE 23:26)

JESUS SHOWS US HOW TO BE
INSTRUMENTS OF GOD'S LOVE

When faced with adversity, some people question God's
fairness. When faced with a serious problem, others

blame their forebears or their peers. When confronted with social problems associated with great poverty, some people withdraw into the comfort and security of their own homes, overwhelmed by their perceived powerlessness. When asked to contribute to a charity or to volunteer their time and talents, still others, enslaved by selfishness, complain that they do not have enough for themselves.

[The Word of God] shed[s] light on the human condition in the face of difficulties and help[s] shape our celebration this morning.

The setting for [Ezekiel 18:25–28] was the Babylonian Exile. While the people of God were languishing in exile, many of them blamed God or their ancestors for their predicament: "Fathers have eaten green [sour] grapes," they complained, "and the children's teeth are on edge." The prophet Ezekiel responds very directly. He points out that each generation receives reward or punishment—life or death—in accord with its own attitudes and actions. God offers each generation all it needs—both to survive adversity and to build a better world, one that reflects the kingdom of God. The important thing is to recognize our God-given individual and collective resources—meager though they may seem—and to use them as wisely and effectively as we can to uproot poverty, eradicate violence, and establish justice, peace, and harmony.

Saint Paul takes a similar tack in his letter to the Philippians [2:1–11]. He calls the community of faith to harmony and unity, offering Christians the selfless example of Jesus. Jesus freely emptied himself from his exalted position and took on the weak human condition. In doing so, he shows us firsthand what we can accomplish when we live in accord with God's will and allow ourselves to be his instruments of love, compassion, and mercy. Paul points out that in order to do this we must take on the attitude of Christ, who is ever obedient to his Father and who came among us filled with enduring, selfless love.

None of this is new to us. In our hearts we know the truth of what Ezekiel and Paul are telling us. . . . But we also know that there is a tension between knowing something and acting on it, there is a difference between saying something and actually doing something about it.

[Matthew's] Gospel takes this problem on directly in the parable of the two sons [21:28–32]—the one who agrees to go to work in the vineyard, as his father suggests, but does not go—and the other one who refuses to go into the vineyard at his father's request but then decides to go. In the context of this passage and in the broader context of Jesus' ministry, the first son resembles the religious leaders of Jesus' day who tripped over their tongues in being the first to say yes to God but then refused to enter into the vineyard, the kingdom of

God proclaimed by Jesus. Tragically, they resisted the new thing God was doing and tenaciously clung to their old traditions. The second son is like the tax collectors and public sinners who at first said no to God. But their encounter with Jesus and their acceptance of his gospel changed their lives. They ultimately entered the vineyard, the kingdom of God.

It is not for us to judge the people of Jesus' time. The same challenge faces us in every generation. Will we say yes to God and work in his vineyard? Or will we refuse or withdraw or try to hide? (September 26, 1993)

God, source of all goodness, there are times when I frankly do not want to work in your vineyard. There are times when, like Simon of Cyrene, I just want to rest awhile rather than help a neighbor with a burden that is not exactly mine. Help me to say yes to your call so that I can help those I encounter on my journey.

FOLLOWING THE LORD DEMANDS STRENGTH AND PERSEVERANCE

The life of discipleship is not an easy one—if we take Jesus for our model [cf. Mark 1:29–39]. After a long day of ministering to hurt and sick people, Jesus has to heal [or help] one more person before he can eat dinner! Afterward there are so many more in need of his healing, comforting touch. When he rises at dawn and retreats to an out-of-the-way place to pray, his disciples seek him out to inform him that everyone is looking for him—again! Discipleship—following the Lord, continuing his ministry—demands strength of character and God-given perseverance. (February 10, 1985)

O God, my shepherd, guide me in your paths. Give me the strength I need to persevere on the journey. But please also lead me beside restful waters at times so that my soul can be refreshed in your presence.

JESUS HELPS US BEAR OUR CROSSES

Jesus invites us to come to him, to learn from him as his disciples. Let us listen again to his beautiful, consoling words: "Come to me, all you who are weary and find life burdensome, and I will refresh you. Take my yoke upon your shoulders and learn from me, for I am gentle and humble of heart. Your souls will find rest, for my yoke is easy and my burden light" [Matthew 11:28–30].

Jesus promises that his yoke will be kind and gentle to our shoulders, enabling us to carry our load more easily. That is what he means when he says his burden is "light." Actually, it might be quite heavy, but we will be able to carry it. Why? Because Jesus himself will help us. It is as though he tells us, "Walk alongside me; learn to carry the burden by observing how I do it. If you let me help you, the heavy labor will seem lighter." (September 14, 1996)

God, my rock, my deliverer, thank you for the example of Simon of Cyrene and the gift of your Son Jesus who helps me carry my burdens. Teach me to walk alongside Jesus and take his yoke upon my shoulders so that, with his help, I can carry my burdens and help others carry theirs.

VERONICA WIPES THE
FACE OF JESUS

Unlike Simon of Cyrene, who was forced to help Jesus,
Veronica evokes a sense of spontaneity, sensitivity and
great compassion when faced with the suffering human
Jesus. It is unsettling to see Jesus so needy on the Way of
the Cross, especially after he has helped so many others with
their diverse needs, turning no one away. But in this Sixth
Station there is both consolation and inspiration when we re-
alize that Veronica offers Jesus some comfort while teaching
us all that we are the risen Lord's eyes, ears and hands on
earth. Cardinal Bernardin truly believed that Christ abides
in us if we walk in his ways. His homilies often stressed
that when we show love and compassion for others, we jour-
ney through life as "ambassadors of Christ." We minister
to others by gestures as simple as listening and as intimate
as picking them up when they fall. Discipleship is an awe-
some task, indeed, but by saying yes to God's grace, we be-
come vessels through which he builds his kingdom.

Come. You have my Father's blessing!
Inherit the kingdom prepared for you from
    the creation of the world.
For I was hungry and you gave me food,
I was thirsty and you gave me drink.
I was a stranger and you welcomed me,
    naked and you clothed me.

I was ill and you comforted me,

in prison and you came to visit me.

(MATTHEW 25:34-36)

✦

GOD'S LOVE MOVES US INTO COURAGEOUS AND CREATIVE SERVICE

My friends, the greatest romance we will ever experience is God's passionate love. The greatest adventure is the journey into his kingdom. The greatest achievement is to live as a faith-filled brother or sister of Jesus, the Savior. The greatest challenge is to carry on Jesus' mission and ministry, incarnating his healing presence and saving love in the world. Through our love for one another, others will experience Immanuel—the fact that God is, indeed, with us.

This means that you and I will have to become the hands and arms of God's love in our world by reaching out to the suffering and marginal people of this metropolitan area, of our nation, of the world. We have to be willing to let the indwelling of God's love move us into courageous and creative service and ministry. The

Word of God challenges us to move beyond fear to hope, beyond paralysis to constructive action, beyond dissension and turmoil to an abiding peace. (December 21, 1986)

Lord God, I am simply in awe of your passionate love for us. It is a mystery that I cannot comprehend and can accept only in faith. Help me to share your love with others, especially those who are needy, those who are most vulnerable, those who are your beloved children and my sisters and brothers.

WE BUILD GOD'S KINGDOM THROUGH OUR DAILY ACTIONS

We build God's kingdom as we strive to put the gospel message into practice in our everyday lives. Through our lives we proclaim the message: God loved us so much that he sent his only Son as our redeemer. Our words may be few, but our deeds ought to proclaim boldly that a close family life is important, that education in our faith is important, that every human being has great dignity in God's eyes, that even the weakest and most helpless among us have rights that need to be respected. We build God's kingdom when we reach out in loving care toward one another, especially toward the sick, the poor, the homeless, the starving. In this way we carry on Jesus' mission, telling the Good News in words and deed.

We need not become discouraged when the progress of God's kingdom among us is not always obvious. God's kingdom grows in secret, like a crop of wheat in the night, like children over the years, like the dawn that slowly overcomes the darkness. God's kingdom is like buried treasure whose value increases with time. The good we do for one another often goes unseen. This should not upset us. Our Heavenly Father sees. It is him we serve. We are not building our own kingdom. He builds his kingdom through us. (November 4, 1984)

God Most Holy, I am curious to know more about Veronica than what is found in the simplicity of this Sixth Station. But it is enough that her example inspires us to do our part each day in building up your kingdom. Please give me the ability to recognize people's needs and help them in whatever ways I can.

We Meet Jesus in Our Intimate
Connection with Others

I need to go out, to experience firsthand the goodness and warmth of our people. Only then can I maintain a correct perspective. But such encounters, I hasten to add, can take a great deal out of you. They can be very draining, both physically and emotionally. But they are worth it, because in those moments—moments of celebration and fellowship—you experience a connectedness that transcends the normal routine of daily life and ministry.

Moreover, the intimate moment that you spend with each person can bring healing and reconciliation into their lives. They experience anew—or for the first time—their authentic self-worth. They may come closer to their parish community and change their attitude about the Church's pastors. They may also enter into a more intimate communion with the Lord himself.

To be with people—simply to be with them in their celebrations and in the course of their daily lives—is no simple task. It may seem a waste of precious time. But we must be willing to expend our time and energy on such occasions. If we constantly look for immediate results and carefully dole out the concern and care we share with the people we encounter, we will not meet

Jesus in them. Further, we will not be able to enjoy and benefit from what *they* have to offer in the exchange, and *we* will not be able to minister to them in an effective and loving way.

The Christian religion is incarnational. Jesus used and enjoyed the normal, simple things of life. He frequently ate and celebrated with his friends—and not only with his close friends but with many of the wider group of people with whom he came into contact. He also chose simple, understandable signs and elements as the basis for the sacramental system. (May 16, 1990)

Heavenly Father, thank you for the example of your Son, Jesus, who was like us in all things but sin. Help me to discover you and the risen Christ in my encounters with others. Let me also be an instrument of your love so that others can experience your presence through my actions.

Seventh Station

JESUS FALLS FOR THE
SECOND TIME

As we saw in the Third Station, falling is a sign of human frailty. While we know that falling is part of the human condition, it often embarrasses us at least or paralyzes us at worst. Once we fall and get back up, we dread ever falling again, for we know that it is more difficult to rise from a second fall. But in the Seventh Station Jesus shows us that getting up again is not only possible but also necessary if we are to embrace our journey through life.

In our own lives there are many ways to fall as we carry our crosses. Having faced the "fall" of the false accusation and gotten up through the power of forgiveness and reconciliation, Cardinal Bernardin was again knocked down—this time by cancer. Again he relied on his faith and came to trust the talents of his doctors to help him get up one more time. In September 1995, three months after he was diagnosed as having cancer and while he was in remission, Cardinal Bernardin was asked to preside at a prayer service in Holy Name Cathedral with priests of the Archdiocese of Chicago. The reason for the service was to thank God for the success of the treatment the cardinal had undergone for pancreatic cancer and to ask God to give him the strength we all need to face difficulties in our lives.

When the just cry out, the LORD hears them . . .
The LORD is close to the brokenhearted;
and those who are crushed in spirit he saves.

Many are the troubles of the just man,

but out of them all the LORD delivers him.

(PSALM 34:18–20)

⁜

WE ENCOUNTER THE CROSS IN
OUR DAILY LIVES

At times when we think about taking up our cross daily, we may first think of the discomforts or problems we face each day. We may think of a chronic illness, a recurring headache, or a digestive problem. We may identify our cross as a difficult person in our lives—a brother or sister, a co-worker, a neighbor. . . .

But when Jesus talks about our daily cross, he is truly referring to the difficulties and obstacles we encounter in striving to live a good Christian life, the opposition we often meet when we live as his faithful disciples. When we live in accord with his gospel, we discover that its message is countercultural—it goes against the stream of conventional human wisdom and culture. . . .

In following Jesus, we walk with him and listen attentively to his word. It is pleasant and comforting to be with him when he heals a blind man, or a deaf woman, or a child who is near death. It is much less comfortable to follow him into the Temple precincts and observe his controversy with the chief priests, the scribes, and the Pharisees.

Similarly, in our personal lives we may find it easy to share our religious faith and moral values with those who agree with us. It is much more difficult to stand firm when our values are tested or attacked, when others encourage us to keep our beliefs and values separate from our work or community life. (March 6, 1994)

Lord, let the light of your countenance shine upon me. I acknowledge my weakness. There are times I do not stand firm when my beliefs or values are tested or attacked. When I fall, please help me get back up. And keep me on the path of your kingdom.

EVEN WHEN WE STUMBLE, WE CAN SERVE GOD

Several years ago, in a conversation I had with several priest friends, I was asked what were my two greatest fears. Without much reflection I told them that I had always had two fears: One was being falsely accused of anything serious; the other was being afflicted with an aggressive type of cancer. Within two years, both occurred!

The first has had a happy ending. [My accuser] Steven Cook and I were reconciled. More important, he was reconciled with the Church. Last week he died peacefully—no longer an angry, alienated man.

The second fear was realized, as you know, this past June. I was feeling great, had many good things planned for the summer, including a vacation. For the first time in my life I was confronted not only with the possibility but also the probability of a premature death. Somehow, with God's grace and the prayers and support of many people, including yourselves, I was able to move beyond the fear; I was able to put aside the unimportant, non-essential things that so often hold us hostage. I was able to see things from a new perspective.

This evening I wish to conclude . . . by telling you how I hope I can be of help to you—personally and ministerially—as together we walk into the future. . . . In the final analysis, my best contribution or gift is to help you grow in the Lord, who alone can bring your efforts to fruition. My best gift to you is *myself*. Beneath the titles of archbishop or cardinal is a man—Joseph Bernardin—who is weak and sinful like you, in need of affirmation and support, at times full of doubts and anxieties, very sensitive, easily hurt and frustrated. But this Joseph is a man of great faith, one who is in love with the Lord, one who struggles each day—sometimes with little obvious success—to decrease so the Lord can increase in him, a man whose life is full of crooked lines but who is willing to let the Lord write straight with them.

Know that this man, Joseph, has a great affection for you. Know that when you fail, he understands. Know that when you do crazy things that bring grief to others (as he himself does so frequently), he forgives you. Know that as you try to cope with the realities of life— both personally and ministerially—he is at your side, ready to help in every way he can. Know that when you succeed, he smiles and shares your joy and satisfaction. Know that when you are sad, hurt, demoralized, he cries with you. Know that this man, Joseph, loves you, that he is proud of you, and that for the sake of the Lord he is ready and willing to give his life for you! (September 25, 1995)

God, Lord Most High, help me to address my fears so that I can let go of them and rely on your great love for me and all your children. I know this will not be easy, but draw me closer to Jesus, who knew human frailty so well and can help me rise from my falls to resume my journey, the journey that leads to peace.

JESUS MEETS
THE WOMEN
OF JERUSALEM

The Eighth Station is perhaps the most difficult of the Stations to understand. Who are these women of Jerusalem? They are not further identified, leaving us with a feeling of mystery and wonder. But it is Jesus' response to these women that is most important. In effect he tells them not to weep for him but to draw a lesson from his fate. Jesus warns that they and their children will also have to contend with the forces of evil. We may reflect on his admonition and recognize more clearly that accompanying Jesus on his journey does not insulate us from the forces of evil.

One of the signs that the forces of evil are at work in and among us is alienation. Cardinal Bernardin had a special gift for overcoming alienation by reconciling people. For example, on a pastoral visit to Poland in 1984 he challenged the people of Bydgoszcz to stand in solidarity with all of God's children in the face of threats by the forces of evil and chaos. He also teaches us to heed Jesus' warning and become better prepared to face the inevitable evil that separates us from God, our true selves, and others on our life's journey.

A great crowd of people followed him, including women who beat their breasts and lamented over him. Jesus turned to them and said: "Daughters of Jerusalem, do not weep for me. Weep for yourselves and for your children. The days are coming when they will say, 'Happy are the sterile, the wombs that never bore and the breasts that never nursed.' Then they will begin saying to the mountains, 'Fall on us,' and to the hills, 'Cover us.' If they do these things in the green wood, what will happen in the dry?"

(LUKE 23:27–31)

WE, TOO, STRUGGLE WITH THE FORCES OF EVIL

We humans are deeply alienated from ourselves and from God, who is the source of all life, when we do not reverence, protect, and promote human life. Abortion; euthanasia; neglect of the poor, the handicapped, and the weak—all these reveal how divided we are from ourselves and others. . . .

We are deeply alienated from ourselves and others when we perpetuate attitudes and structures that divide people on the basis of racial and cultural differences. Racism—in whatever form—keeps us away from each other, keeps us strangers to each other and even strangers to our very selves. . . .

When I step back from these particular situations that I have so briefly indicated, I see a pattern emerging. Again, please believe me: I do not credit myself with special cleverness. No. Rather, I see God's hand at work, inspiring and sustaining my best efforts, as indeed he does yours. I see six steps.

The *first* involves coming to know the *fact and roots* of human alienation, whatever the form. This is not necessarily pleasant or easy, but it is absolutely necessary. In general, it means that I must learn to *listen deeply* so as to grasp fully the realities involved.

A *second* step is to *renew my commitment* to serve healing reconciliation, to be a willing instrument for it, whatever this demands. I must confess that I often become discouraged. I can continue to serve only by continually renewing my commitment to work for reconciliation.

A *third* step is to *identify and engage resources* to help me. I must humbly—that is to say, honestly—recognize that I do not have the wherewithal to address all the issues I confront. I depend on others; I depend on institutions; I depend on so much.

A *fourth* step is to *risk taking initiatives*. In other words, I must *do something*.

A *fifth* step is to *trust God*. I must surrender; I must entrust myself to God totally. In this I recognize that the work of reconciliation is not mine but God's, that I serve reconciliation in a real but instrumental way.

The *final* step is to *hold fast*. It is not enough to make attempts, to take risks, to start something and then walk away. Our fidelity must follow the pattern set by the Lord. He will not let us stay alienated. He continues to knock, to invite, and to call us to a healed life *at home* with him and with one another.

Consider your own ministry and life. Become familiar with the patterns unique to you. Probe the ways that God has worked in and through *you*. (May 15, 1990)

Creator God, who made order out of chaos, help me to recognize the forces of evil and chaos that threaten to overwhelm me at times. Send your Holy Spirit to guide me so that I can learn the truth about myself, about others, about the world. Let me hear well Jesus' advice to the women of Jerusalem and help me hold fast to your path, even in shaky times.

WE STAND WITH ONE ANOTHER AS CHILDREN OF GOD

Jesus challenges us in the Gospels: "Get hold of yourselves! . . . Do not be afraid!" (Mark 6:50). Our strength

and courage come from the Lord. No matter how difficult the struggle, no matter how discouraged we might
become in the face of opposition, the Lord is with us.
We also stand with one another as brothers and sisters,
children of the same God. (August 12, 1984)

*O God, I take refuge in you. Please manifest your
presence in my life so that I will know that I do not
walk alone. And help me to stand in solidarity with
the women of Jerusalem—with all of your children—so that we will remain steadfast in our encounters with the forces of chaos that tend to
overwhelm us.*

Ninth Station

JESUS FALLS FOR THE THIRD TIME

*The end is near. Jesus is exhausted. This third fall is the
most difficult, the hardest to overcome. Death is imminent—
the ultimate "falling down." But Jesus' journey of the
Cross and the glory that lies behind it cannot end here. He
must get up one more time before his mission is complete.*

*As the following selections reveal, Cardinal Bernardin
believed that having faith means embracing the Cross as
fully as possible. He knew the difficulties, but he believed
that we never embrace the Cross alone, that God never
abandons us. Five weeks before he died, the cardinal spoke
to the priests of the Archdiocese of Chicago at a prayer
service and shared with them that his lifelong struggle to
understand Jesus and his expectations had culminated in
the ability to let go, to surrender himself fully to God. The
result was that Joseph Bernardin experienced a deep inner
peace that allowed him to see death as a friend, not an
enemy. For, as Jesus teaches us, inherent in the pain of the
Cross is the joy of everlasting peace.*

I am like water poured out;
    all my bones are racked.
My heart has become like wax
    melting away within my bosom.

My throat is dried up like baked clay,
    my tongue cleaves to my jaws;

to the dust of death you have brought

    me down.

(PSALM 22:15–16)

✤

THE CROSS IS DIFFICULT BUT
ALSO SWEET AND EASY

[T]he Cross . . . is a symbol of suffering and death as well as victory. The Cross, in so many ways, is reflective of life—both its agonies and its ecstasies. For the person of faith, despite all the suffering, it is ultimately both the symbol and cause of victory. In recent months the Cross, my brothers, has never been more difficult or sweeter to me.

My spiritual journey goes back for many years. But it did not really begin to take shape until I learned, with my heart as well as my mind, who Jesus is and what he expects of me. The answers to these two questions came over a period of time, through study of the Scriptures, prayer, exchanges with my fellow priests—and my ministerial experiences—but especially through prayer and the Scriptures. It is both the discovery and the internalization of the answer to those two questions that have given me the strength to carry the cross that Jesus has given me the privilege to share with him.

My brothers, I am in the midst of this "letting go." It is like the Cross: Sometimes it is sweet and easy, sometimes very difficult. My faith is unwavering. It shapes my mind and will and keeps me on the right track. But human emotions can be quite fickle, as all of you so well know. But there is no reason to hide those emotions. In no way is there a contradiction between them and our faith and trust. (October 7, 1996)

God, my Redeemer, I may not yet have had direct experience of this "third fall," but I know others who have. Give me the strength I need to keep getting up, even as I learn how to let go. May your Spirit guide me along the way that leads to peace.

We Are Created for the Light of God's Love

If you accept the Lord's peace into your hearts, the darkness will not be able to overwhelm you. There is nothing that you and God cannot face together. God's love revealed in Jesus is the most powerful force the universe will ever know. All the heartbreak, misery, and suffering cannot overcome his love. Reach for it! Accept it into your heart! (Feast of the Holy Family, 1986)

God, my Savior, deepen my faith and trust in your love for me. I believe that, with your help, I can face any obstacle on my pilgrim way. But that does not mean that I have lost all my fears, lack of confidence and anxiety. So please be patient with me, and give me the strength I need each day.

GOD WILL NEVER ABANDON US

Meaghan was as lost as a little four-year-old could possibly be. Shopping for Christmas dinner was turning out to be an unhappy affair! Her daddy had warned her about being too slow, but she had dawdled by the frozen food case—she wanted to see her breath—and spent at least five minutes in the cereal aisle trying to read the back of a Cap'n Crunch box. By the time she skipped into the produce department, her father was nowhere in sight. So she sat down by the bananas and began to cry.

When a stock boy asked her what was wrong, she repeated her name, address, and telephone number—

just as her daddy had taught her to do if she ever got lost. It wasn't as good as seeing her father, but it made her feel better. By the time she finally saw him running around the corner, she had repeated her name, address, and telephone number to the produce manager, three stock boys, a cashier, and four senior citizens.

When she saw her daddy, her courage melted like the chocolate bar she had been given by the store manager. Her father picked her up in his strong arms and said, "Meaghan, princess, I'm sorry I lost you!" And Meaghan, through her tears, sobbed, "Daddy, I'm sorry you lost me, too!"

Everyone laughed and then applauded. And then her father promised he would never lose her again— and you know, he never did! Daddies are like that.

Basically, that is the promise that our Heavenly Father makes to us. He promises us, here and now, once and forever, that he will *never* abandon us. Think about that! The Lord will never lose us.

His promise is not theoretical, pious, or superficial. It's real. It's living. And it's made to you and me.

His promise, his Word, takes flesh and dwells among us. We know him by many names and titles. Jesus, Immanuel—God is with us now and always. Jesus— the one sent to save us from our sins.

Why is this such Good News? Because, like Meaghan, like the generations of Christians who have preceded us, we are the people who seek the face of God. Left to ourselves, we find that we are nothing, powerless, helpless, empty, parched with thirst, racked with hunger for something more.

Our age is no different from others in this regard. But the hunger and thirst for something more—something deeper, something that gives meaning and focus to our busy lives—may have become more intense for us. And this is as it should be, for, as Saint Augustine observed so insightfully, "You have made us for yourself, O Lord, and our hearts are restless until they find their rest in you" [*Confessions*, 1, 1]. (December 21, 1986)

Heavenly Father, it is consoling to know that you will never lose or abandon any of your children. As I meditate on the Ninth Station of the Cross, I have a deeper sense of the significance of this assurance. When my heart is restless, I know now why this is so: because the rest, the peace, I seek can be found only in you.

JESUS IS STRIPPED OF HIS GARMENTS

Having gotten up one last time, Jesus comes to the end of the road. We watch as he now stands on Calvary, stripped naked before a hostile crowd while Roman soldiers gamble for his garb. On one hand this is the ultimate humiliation. On the other hand, standing naked before the Lord means being honest and humble, holding nothing back from him. Difficult? Yes, but not impossible for a true believer.

Cardinal Bernardin was very sensitive to the ways in which people denigrate and discount one another. He understood that humiliation can be caused on grand scales and in subtle ways. A constant message throughout his life was that the journey of faith calls us to be our truest, best selves so that we can be a light for others and the world. When life strips us of everything, faith clothes us in God's acceptance and love.

After the soldiers had crucified Jesus they took his garments and divided them four ways, one for each soldier. There was also his tunic, but this tunic was woven in one piece from top to bottom and had no seam. They said to each other, "We should not tear it. Let us throw dice to see who gets it." (The purpose of this was to have the Scripture fulfilled: "they divided my garments among them; for my clothing they cast lots.") And this was what the soldiers did.

(JOHN 19:23–24)

A friend of mine brought back a book of photographs that he bought [at Yad Vashem in Jerusalem]. Its title is *The Holocaust* [and it was published by the Martyrs and Heroes Remembrance Authority at Yad Vashem.] The caption of the first photo describes a "Nazi mass rally in Berlin (August 15, 1936) at which they foresaw a Germany 'cleansed' of Jews." The chief slogan in this picture reads, "The Jews are our misfortune."

The final photo in the book bears this caption: "Children—prisoners of the Auschwitz concentration camp—after liberation (January 1945)". . . .

I would like to share with you some reflections based on one photo from that book. It is not the most horrible picture, nor is it the most famous. Let me describe it for you and then share some of my own reactions and reflections.

Two men face one another. One is a Nazi soldier. The other a Jewish civilian. The Nazi wears a steel helmet with the strap secured tightly under his prominent chin. The civilian wears a cloth cap with a billed visor. The soldier's mouth looks as if it is just about to break into a grin. He seems to be enjoying what he is doing. By contrast, the Jewish civilian's face is contorted, twisted, as if he is about to weep. There is great pain, grief, agony, embarrassment in his countenance. In his right hand the soldier has a pair of scissors—not a weapon. He is cutting off the beard and earlocks of the Jewish believer.

The caption reads, "Shearing off or plucking out beard and earlocks of Orthodox Jews in front of jeering crowds was a favorite pastime in occupied Poland."

Why does that picture remain in my mind? On the surface it is far more benign than the pictures of emaciated bodies lying strewn in a huge mass grave in the Nordhausen concentration camp. It is not as confronting as the eighteen faces staring from the wooden bunks at Buchenwald. It is not as gruesome as the skeletal remains outside the crematorium furnaces of Majdanek. . . .

Why then does it stand out? Because it is so close to being ordinary. Because it is not so horrendous as to be totally alien to our own experience. Because it is within the realm of our own possibilities for cruelty.

. . . So many of the perpetrators of the horrors of the Holocaust were banal, petty, mean-spirited, envious, cruel people. They were bullies who had extraordinary opportunity to act out their prejudices, their hatreds.

That is what we see in the picture that I just described. A bully who has power over another human being. A person who can transform a simple act that barbers perform daily into an act of humiliation and desecration. How simple it is to cut someone's hair! And yet what a violation of one's dignity it can be. What a violation of a sacred way of life, a faith, a tradition, a commitment! A smirk on one face. Depth of pain, loss, humiliation on the other. . . .

As we look at this scene, we realize that we are, at our worst moments, capable of similar actions. No, we could not starve people to death. No, we would not turn on a gas oven or crematorium. No, we could not shoot children in cold blood. But yes, we could humiliate another human person. Yes, we could smirk in enjoyment at someone else's embarrassment. Yes, we could mock someone else's cherished symbols of belief.

The child who taunts a classmate beyond endurance. The adult who tells jokes with racial, religious, or ethnic mockery. The superior who publicly berates an employee. These commonplace instances are not entirely alien to the banality, the petty cruelty, the meanness of spirit in that photograph.

. . . Two men face to face. One with a pair of scissors and a smug grin. He is in command. The other with shorn locks and deep pain. That is what we see on the surface of things. But the words of the Book of Lamentations help us see beneath the surface:

I tell myself my future is lost . . .

But I will call this to mind,

as my reason to have hope . . .

My portion is the LORD . . .

therefore will I hope in him.

(LAMENTATIONS 3:18, 21, 24)

The magnificence of faith and goodness stands triumphant over the banality of evil and malice. The Holocaust recalls, at one and the same time, the depths to which humanity can fall and the heights to which human beings can rise. In the final analysis, love is stronger than death. Faith is stronger than hatred. Compassion will outlast cruelty. (April 15, 1988)

O God, my shield and my protector, I know what it means to have power over someone else. It is a human weakness to strive for power over others; it alienates us from our true selves and from others. Help me to cleanse this weakness from my life so that I can help empower others, not humiliate them.

We must first relax—physically and emotionally. We must quiet the noise in our hearts. We must be *still*. We have to get away from our ministerial duties, our co-workers, the pressures and frustrations that are part of the daily cross we carry.

Then we must stand before the Lord, *naked*, without any kind of camouflage, make-believe, or pretense. We must leave our outer mask at the door. As public persons, this isn't always easy to do, as you and I well know.

We must also be *open* to whatever he has in mind for us; we must be willing to take whatever path he points out. Otherwise, there would be little point in coming together this way. Our journey into the wilderness would end up being merely an intellectual exercise, without impacting our life and ministry in any significant way. The only ground rule is that nothing in our life—good, bad, or indifferent—can be off-limits to the Lord.

Finally, we must signal our willingness to be *converted* more deeply, more completely. We must be willing to accept his transforming love. Ultimately, this is a matter of the heart. "Oh, that today you would hear his voice: 'Harden not your hearts as at Meribah, as in the day of Massah in the desert,

Where your fathers tempted me;
they tested me though they had seen my works.' "
(Psalm 95:7–9). (May 14, 1990)

> *O Lord, my God, it is difficult to stand or sit or
> kneel in your presence just as I am, with no pre-
> tenses, no camouflage. It is even harder to allow you
> to guide me on my journey; I often prefer to chart
> my own course. Help me to listen to you so that I
> may truly give my heart to you, holding nothing
> back.*

CONVERSION DEMANDS THAT WE BE HUMBLE AND HONEST

Conversion . . . demands certain things of us. First, it demands a certain *humility*. By this, I mean knowing who *we* are and who *Jesus* is. It means being truthful, honest with ourselves and with Jesus. Much of our time is spent pretending, trying to persuade others and even ourselves that we are different from what we really are. But how can we talk about conversion unless we acknowledge our *true* rather than our *imaginary* selves? How can we enter into an authentic relationship with the Lord if it is not based on honesty and truthfulness?

How can Jesus help us, heal us, reconcile us if we are unwilling to present ourselves to him as we are? When we turn to the Lord in conversion, we need not be afraid to tell him about our failings, our infidelities, our sins. He understands us better than we do ourselves. So all we need is to acknowledge candidly our strengths and weaknesses—in fact, our total dependence on him. (October 13, 1984)

God, you are my light and my salvation. Help me to be honest with myself. That is true humility, not puffing myself up or discounting the gifts I have received from you. You already know all about me. Why do I try to hide from you? Why do I not trust you more?

JESUS IS NAILED TO THE CROSS

As if the journey to the Cross has not been painful enough, Jesus is subjected to the cruelty of crucifixion. A violent, torturous way to die, it is nearly impossible to witness— even in our culture of violence. Yet, as Cardinal Bernardin helps us see, when we view the crucifixion through the eyes of faith, we become witnesses to the sealing of the New Covenant in Jesus' blood. Suddenly we hear Jesus' words of forgiveness toward those who have crucified him, and we stop in our tracks, because we know how difficult forgiveness and reconciliation can be. We stretch our arms wide, like Jesus, and open our entire being to God and others.

When they came to Skull Place, as it was called, they crucified him there and the criminals as well, one on his right and the other on his left. [Jesus said, "Father, forgive them; they do not know what they are doing."] . . . It was now around midday, and darkness came over the whole land until midafternoon with an eclipse of the sun.

(LUKE 23:33–34a, 44)

The New Covenant Is Sealed
with Jesus' Blood

In the covenant God promises to take care of his people as a shepherd cares for his flock. The people, on their part, take on the responsibilities of observing God's law, which in turn teaches them how to live in right relationships with him and with one another. The covenant is sealed with blood. For the ancient Israelites, blood symbolized life. The blood of sacrifice was poured on the altar—symbolizing God—and sprinkled on the people. In effect, it gave visible expression to the fact that *new* life now flowed between God and his people, between God and his human family.

In the *new* and *eternal* covenant, through the death and resurrection of Jesus, we are made into a new people, a new creation. As in the former covenant, we are called upon to love God with all that we are and to love our neighbor as ourself. This new and eternal covenant is sealed with the very blood of Jesus, poured out on the Cross and offered daily on our altars. New life flows between God and his people. (June 9, 1985)

God, source of all life, blood is a precious sub-
stance in our world that is too often spilled and
wasted in violence. But the Precious Blood of your
Son Jesus seals our covenant with you and allows
new life to flow between you and your people. Help
me to become more aware of the value of each
human life, from conception to natural death and
in all its circumstances.

JESUS PRACTICED WHAT HE PREACHED

[The reading from Saint Luke's Gospel (6:27–38)] . . .
places before us one of Jesus' key challenges: "Love
your enemies, do good to those who hate you. . . .
When someone slaps you on one cheek, turn and give
him the other." Jesus himself practiced what he
preached. As he lay in agony, his head crowned with
thorns that pierced his skin, as he twisted in agony while
the hammer beat the nails deeper and deeper into the
tendons of his wrists, he still was able to utter those
amazing words: "Father, forgive them for they know
not what they do." He loved his enemies to the very
end. He did good to those who hated him. He not only
challenged us to this profound dimension of love, but
he showed us the way.

Sometimes it seems easier to love our enemies if they are distant. The farther away people are, the less we see them, the easier it is to forgive and forget. But the persons who are close to us, whose lives are entwined with our own, whose words and idiosyncrasies grate on us day after day—these are the greatest challenges because time and space do not insulate us from those actions, words, memories, or hurts that cause us pain or resentment.

To love the members of our own family is an ongoing task. To love our next-door neighbor is, at times, also not easy. To love our fellow parishioners is a persistent challenge. (February 23, 1992)

God of mercy and compassion, we are learning that forgiving does not mean forgetting, but rather remembering so that we will not allow the hurt to be repeated. At the same time, I find it difficult to forgive others and even myself. Help me to learn from the example of my crucified Lord how to truly forgive.

JESUS SHOWS US HOW TO KEEP
OUR FOCUS ON GOD'S PURPOSE

Jesus' ministry is not orderly, but we would hardly suggest that it has no focus. He is frequently overextended in ministering to those in need but never loses his way. His work at times interferes with his sleep but not with his prayer. For years I wondered how he kept his ministry so clearly on track through all the interruptions and obstacles—all the "mess" of the world that intruded into his life and work.

Then one day it struck me that when Jesus opened his arms to embrace a little child and when he opened his arms wide on the Cross to embrace the whole world, it was one and the same. He came among us "filled with enduring love" (John 1:14). So the people he encountered on his journeys were never interruptions, distractions, or obstacles. For him they were *opportunities* to carry out his mission; this is why the Father sent him into the world! (May 15, 1990)

O Lord, my God, it is so easy for me to lose my way during each day's hustle and bustle. I set out with the intention of living in your presence and walking in your ways, but there are so many distractions, so many choices, so much noise in my life! Help me to carry out Jesus' mission, using every interruption and distraction as an opportunity to proclaim Jesus and his gospel in all I say and do.

Conversion Demands That We Be Open to God

Conversion demands that we be *open* to what the Lord wants of us. We have to be willing to become instruments in his hands. We must be willing—indeed, eager—to incarnate in our lives the paschal mystery, the dying and rising of Jesus. Saint Paul is a marvelous model for those who wish to be successful evangelizers. Throughout his letter he emphasizes the changes that occur in him as his union with the Lord deepens. He tells the Colossians, "In my own flesh I fill up what is lacking in the sufferings of Christ for the sake of his body, the church" (Colossians 1:24). And to the Galatians, "I have been crucified with Christ, and the life I live now is not my own; Christ is living in me" (Galatians 2:19–20). When we are open to the Lord's expectations of us, we become one with him. We become the instruments through which he showers his love, mercy, and healing on the human family. (October 13, 1984)

God, it is difficult enough to see my Lord nailed to a cross. It is positively terrifying to say that I have been crucified with him! Help me to embrace the Cross each day and to be united with my crucified Lord so that I may also be united one day with the risen Lord.

Twelfth Station

JESUS DIES ON

THE CROSS

It is not easy to stand before the Cross, and the evangelists knew this. The Gospel of Mark does not say that anyone close to Jesus was there on Calvary that afternoon. The Gospel of Matthew notes that many women, who had followed Jesus from Galilee, were present, "looking on from a distance" (Matthew 27:55). The Gospel of Luke is similar: "All his friends and the women who had accompanied him from Galilee were standing at a distance watching everything" (Luke 23:49). It seems safer, somehow easier to stand off in the distance to observe Jesus' death. But we are invited to stand up close with his mother, a few other women, and his beloved disciple.

Cardinal Bernardin often invited people to come closer to the Cross, to witness every aspect of it. In August 1982 he issued this invitation to his priests on the night before his installation as Archbishop of Chicago. In August 1984 he invited the pilgrims at Częstochowa to embrace the Cross. And five weeks before he died, he invited his priests to stand at the foot of the Cross and be converted by the intimacy with Jesus.

Near the cross of Jesus there stood his mother, his mother's sister, Mary, the wife of Clopas, and Mary Magdalene. Seeing his mother there with the disciple whom he loved, Jesus said to his mother, "Woman, there is your son." In turn he said to the disciple, "There is your mother." From that hour onward, the disciple took her into his care.

After that, Jesus, realizing that everything was now finished, said to fulfill the Scripture, "I am thirsty." There was a jar there, full of common wine. They stuck a sponge soaked in this wine on some hyssop and raised it to his lips. When Jesus took the wine, he said, "Now it is finished." Then he bowed his head, and delivered over his spirit.

(JOHN 19:25–30)

LET US STAND WITH MARY BEFORE THE CROSS

[Mary] is present [to us] similar to the way she stood at the foot of the Cross. She is present in faith, hope, and love. Because she loves her children as she loved her own Son, Mary provides a consoling, healing presence among her sons and daughters. We come to her with our bruises, our cuts, and our inner hurts, knowing that she is an understanding Mother, who cares for us.

She is as a believer, as someone who has put all her trust in God and dedicated her whole being to carrying out his will. When she gave her *fiat* and became the

Mother of Jesus, the rest of her life was devoted to the person and the work of her Son. Because she believed and because she responded obediently to the Word that God addressed to her, she became the new Eve, the new Mother of all the living. . . .

Mary stands before the Cross . . . as a loving Mother who suffers with her children. She stands at the Cross with hope for the future in her heart. As the Mother of the Church, she reminds us that God never abandons his people. He has promised a kingdom of justice and harmony, of peace and solidarity. He is all-powerful and can bring about what he promises. He is faithful to his word and will fulfill what he has promised. He has sent his only Son among us, "filled with enduring love" (John 1:14). Mary stands before the Cross knowing that from this suffering and Cross will come resurrection and the Kingdom.

Let us stand with Mary before the Cross, learning from her how we might become people of such faith, hope, and love. (August 14, 1984)

My God, my God, how awesome it is to stand at the foot of the Cross with Mary and see your Son die. He is the New Adam who has said yes to you, and his Mother is the New Eve. Saying yes to you, even to the moment of death, is essential to a beloved disciple, I believe, but please help me to say it and mean it.

By Standing at the Foot of the Cross, We Say Yes to God

As we stand at the foot of the Cross—a difficult place to be for every generation, especially our own—we are immediately struck by Jesus' extreme suffering on our behalf. In an age like our own, marked in part by the quest for instant relief from suffering, it takes special courage and determination to stand on Calvary.

But standing at the foot of the Cross teaches us something very profound. What ultimately counts is that we say yes to what God requires of us, no matter how costly it may be. It is essential that we not be sidetracked from our mission—from the Church's mission—by financial problems, inner fear, the hostility of others, or unwarranted harassment. Uniting our suffering with that of Jesus, we receive strength and courage, a new lease on life, and undaunted hope for the future.

I'm no different from you. If I have succeeded in my ministry, it's *not* because of my human qualities. I do have some gifts and talents, of course, just as you do. But I also have many weaknesses and anxieties. Sin has been and continues to be part of my life, as I'm sure it is of yours.

What is important for you and me is that—if we

allow it—our weakness can become our strength. For when we acknowledge our weakness, we're more inclined to turn to Jesus, we're more willing to give ourselves over to him so that he can work *in* and *through* us. And when we are in touch with the weakness and suffering in our own lives—and in those of our people— we're drawn to stand at the foot of the Cross and learn about the redemptive value of Jesus' suffering and ours. (May 18, 1990)

> *Lord God, I am exhausted by the journey so far. The Twelfth Station at first seems to be the culmination, the summit of the Way of the Cross. But I know there is more, and there is much more I need to learn. Help me to better understand the redemptive value of suffering.*

INTIMACY WITH THE LORD DEMANDS RADICAL CHANGES

Conversion [demands that] we have the *courage* actually to allow Jesus to take over every part of our life. True conversion means total commitment to the Lord. It means entrusting our entire life into his hands, holding nothing back from him. It does not exempt any part of our lives. This courage enables us to take the risks that such intimacy always involves when we allow some-one—the Lord, in this case—to enter our life fully and without reservations. When we become intimate with anyone, our life and our decisions are no longer simply our own. That is why intimacy with the Lord Jesus can be dangerous! It can demand radical changes of us. But as you know so well, the fruits of this intimacy are worth far more than the risks! (October 13, 1984)

God, the rock of my heart, it is difficult to continue standing on Calvary. Its meaning is seeping deeper into my being, inviting me into closer intimacy with my crucified Lord. I know it means I have to make changes in my life. Send your Spirit to guide me and give me the courage and strength I need.

My Greatest Hope

Fourteen years ago, when I was first introduced to you the evening before the formal installation [as Arch-bishop of Chicago], I said,

As our lives and ministries are mingled together through the breaking of the Bread and the blessing of the Cup, I hope that long before my name falls from the eucharistic prayer in the silence of death, you will know well who I am. You will know because we will work and play together, fast and pray together, mourn and rejoice together, despair and hope together, dispute and be reconciled together. You will know me as a friend, fellow priest, and bishop. You will know also that I love you. For I am Joseph, your brother!

That moment of silence will soon be here. I pray that my initial hope has been realized. (October 7, 1996)

Lord, my God, my life is mingled with those of my brothers and sisters in the faith who share with me the Body and Blood of Christ. The Eucharist is both the sign and the source of our unity, our communion, our solidarity. This is a great mystery, but it is also the basis of my hope for the future.

JESUS IS TAKEN DOWN FROM THE CROSS

The Thirteenth Station is shrouded in darkness and enveloped in an eerie silence. It is a time of sadness. But it is also a moment for quiet contemplation. As Mary cradles the lifeless body of her son on her lap, we are reminded of the importance of family, in good times and in hard times. Michelangelo's statue the Pietà *eloquently sums up the emotion of the moment—grief over loss, maternal love that extends beyond death, relief that Jesus' suffering is finally over.*

The scene of this Station also helps us connect what has just happened with our own lives, with the world in which we live. As Cardinal Bernardin reminds us, we are part of the holy family of God that transforms the darkness into light. It is an overwhelming challenge to carry on Jesus' ministry and mission—especially in the face of violence, suffering, death and loss—but we need not attempt it alone. The risen Lord will be with us, and the Spirit of God will guide and empower us.

There were also women present looking on from a distance. Among them were Mary Magdalene, Mary the mother of James the younger and Joses, and Salome. These women had followed Jesus when he was in Galilee and attended to his needs. There were also many others who had come up with him to Jerusalem.

As it grew dark (it was Preparation Day, that

is, the eve of the Sabbath), Joseph from Arimathea arrived—a distinguished member of the Sanhedrin. He was another who looked forward to the reign of God. He was bold enough to seek an audience with Pilate and urgently requested the body of Jesus. Pilate was surprised that Jesus should have died so soon. He summoned the centurion and inquired whether Jesus was already dead. Learning from him that he was dead, Pilate released the corpse to Joseph. Then, having brought a linen shroud, Joseph took him down, and wrapped him in the linen.

(MARK 15:40–46a)

WE ARE ALL PART OF THE HOLY FAMILY OF GOD

Paul's letter to the Colossians (3:12–21) tells us that love [within a family] is not something beyond our reach. It is kind, humble, meek, patient. It *forgives;* it avoids bitterness; it is obedient; it does not nag. That kind of love is painful; it is never cheap. The real thing *costs* something, but the price must not deter us.

In writing of the Holy Family, Father Walter Burghardt, S.J.—a well-known writer and friend of mine—wrote:

> One day Jesus and Mary folded the lifeless hands of Joseph on his breast—and loneliness lay over Nazareth. One spring afternoon Mary waved to her Son as he disappeared round the bend, bound for souls and a cross at the end; one spring afternoon the mother, who first cradled the naked body of her baby in a stable, last cradled that same naked body beneath a cross—and loneliness lay over Jerusalem. And one lonely evening the Mother of God, grown old as gracefully as the petals fall from the rose, left this earth; and the Son, who had come to her without pain, without pain folded her forever to his sacred breast.

All of us have families, but some of us are not with them. Death may have taken a beloved spouse, or children may have moved away to start their own families. Others may have chosen not to marry, but they are not with us. However, whether united or separated, all of us are part of that holy family of God. (December 26, 1982)

God, Creator of all, it is very moving to stand near
Jesus' mother, Mary, as she holds the body of her
dead son before allowing it to be prepared for burial.
So many people die or are killed with no family
present to console them or to embrace their bodies
afterward. Help me to understand—and act accord-
ingly—that everyone I encounter belongs to your
holy family and is my sister or brother.

JESUS CRUCIFIED IS A WINDOW ON OUR WORLD AND A MIRROR FOR OURSELVES

A small community of women and a man circled the foot of the Cross to be with Jesus in his Passion. More at a distance, other women and men stood and watched. Matthew's account states, "Many women were present looking on from a distance. They had *followed* Jesus from Galilee to attend to his needs" (Matthew 27:55) [emphasis added].

[But Matthew 27:45–54] holds before us the crucified Jesus and invites us to draw close, to look intently, and to believe. And in doing so, we find *life*.

- To draw close
- To look with faith
- To respond to the need that is seen . . .

That was the way of that early band of believers. And that is also [our] way.

Do you see the account of the crucified son of Joseph and Mary as a "window" on our world and a "mirror" for ourselves?

Do you see in the body broken and the blood poured out an expression of the passion and compassion of God?

Do you see the darkness that descends upon the whole countryside as both a foreshadowing of the darkness of our own day as well as the creative atmosphere in which God secretly weaves our salvation?

Can you imagine the earth quaking . . . ? Can you see the boulders splitting and the tombs releasing their prisoners—a work that the Cross, driven into the resistant earth, has accomplished?

Do you detect the seismic rumblings of our own day that are both the pains of labor and the promise of life?

Do you see in your own struggles . . . a participation in God's passion and compassion that bonds you to one another and to all who suffer and struggle?

I sense that you do see all these things—and much more. That is why we have much to celebrate in [the] Eucharist.

. . . Your experience . . . in the Church and in the world gives you a "window" on the struggles . . . of all people. And by holding the mirror up to your own experiences in Christ, you draw near to the Passion, to the Cross, which opens onto the fullness of life.

Women are raising their prophetic voice in response to injustices in Church and in society. It is a voice that is strong, imaginative, and much needed. It has great power. . . . What if a *community* of [faith] raised their voices in communion with other women and men of faith? The earth would still quake, the boulders split, and the tombs open before the truth spoken in love.

. . . The prophetic voice is ultimately one of *compassion,* not condemnation. God chooses women and men to raise their voices as an alarm to awaken the world to the destructiveness of its ways. God calls them to express the divine longing that all draw nearer, that all turn back. One of the realities that we celebrate in [the] Eucharist is the presence here of a prophetic spirit that is both passionate and compassionate.

What is more, we offer to God your identity as a community of believers. Your prayer together generates an atmosphere of support and challenge that breathes life into the various ministries and services that you have undertaken. That is an important witness for laity and clergy alike, as we all seek to understand the necessary community dimension of our Catholic Faith.

. . . How crucial are the choices that we make! How

important that our discernments be choices for light and not darkness, for life and not death! (March 13, 1988)

Almighty God, to enter into the scene of the Thirteenth Station is at first to experience helplessness in the face of death, especially the violent death of an innocent person. But as I stand here, I am reminded that I, too, have a mission—to carry on Jesus' own mission and ministry, transforming darkness into light. Most important, I resolve to make choices for life and light, not death and darkness. Help me to do this!

WE ARE GOD'S INSTRUMENTS OF LIGHT WHO DISPEL DARKNESS

The recognition that life is a precious but also fragile gift generates both a sense of responsibility and specific obligations. Human life is not meant to be lived in isolation from others. In our increasingly interdependent world, no one truly lives alone. Rather, we live on various levels of human community, called both to defend our brothers' and sisters' right to life and to work toward enhancing the quality of their lives.

We must create an atmosphere within our society, a

climate in which the value and sanctity of human life are acknowledged, affirmed, and defended. Moreover, we must be consistent in our respect for and protection of human life at every stage and in every circumstance. A commitment to human dignity and human rights requires protection of human life from conception until natural death. It also requires a constant effort to assure every person a fullness of opportunity and a legitimate share in the material benefits and advantages of the modern world.

My dear brothers and sisters, who will bring light to dispel the darkness of our world? If not you and me, then *who*? And if not now, today, then *when*?

Let us carefully heed and generously respond to the word of God:
"I will make you a light to the nations,
that my salvation may reach to the ends of the earth"
(Isaiah 49:6a).
We are the instruments God uses to dispel the world's darkness. There are no others. So even if what we can do might seem insignificant, our effort is needed. Let us, then, live up to our responsibility! (January 17, 1993)

God of light and life, it is difficult to resume our journey when someone beloved has been taken from our midst. We know that our lives will never be the same. It is time to begin the transition, however, to the next phase of our journey. Send your Spirit to enable me to protect and defend, nurture and enhance every human life I encounter. Help me to be a light to the nations!

JESUS IS LAID
IN THE TOMB

The Gospel of John is quite striking in the way it weaves
together the narratives of Jesus' raising of Lazarus from
the dead with Jesus' own imminent death. The theological
thread that binds these stories together is the belief that
Jesus is both resurrection and life. As Cardinal Bernardin
frequently pointed out, the risen Lord can not only help us
rise from the graves we dig for ourselves but also enable us
to help others rise from theirs. If we allow the Spirit of God
to be active in our lives, to transform us, we call each other
from our self-made graves and become living community. In
turn, we transform the world.

[Joseph of Arimathea] laid [Jesus' body] in a tomb
hewn out of the rock, in which no one had yet
been buried.

That was the Day of Preparation, and the sabbath was about to begin. The women who had
come with him from Galilee followed along behind. They saw the tomb and how his body was
buried. Then they went home to prepare spices
and perfumes. They observed the sabbath as a day
of rest, in accordance with the law.

(LUKE 23:53–56)

[The Gospel of Saint John (11:1–44)] focuses on the theme of life and death. Jesus learns that his beloved friend, Lazarus, is seriously ill, but he waits two days before setting out for Bethany, where Lazarus lived. When he begins this journey, Jesus knows that Lazarus is dead. The trip apparently takes three days, for Jesus is informed upon his arrival in Bethany that Lazarus has been dead for four days. Nevertheless, he raises Lazarus from the dead and restores him to life. That is the story in a nutshell. But it lacks some very important details—especially Jesus' conversation with Martha, Lazarus' sister.

Like Martha and the bystanders, we may also wonder why Jesus delayed in going to Bethany until after he knew that Lazarus had already died. Jesus has the reputation of being a powerful healer of various kinds of illnesses. However, the basic thrust of this chapter in Saint John's Gospel is its message that Jesus is both the resurrection and the life—for all who, like Martha, believe in him. Faith enables a person who has died to live with God forever. One who has faith will never truly die—that is, he or she will never be separated from God. That is a powerful, consoling message.

But there is a deeper significance to this narrative. When Jesus gives new life to his friend Lazarus, he risks losing his own life. Bethany is only two miles from Jerusalem, where Jesus' enemies live. As a matter of fact, at the very end of this narrative about the raising of Lazarus, the chief priests and the Pharisees met to decide what to do about Jesus. Their conclusion was that he must die.

SO THE SHADOW OF THE Cross falls across the joy and jubilation of the raising of Lazarus from the dead. Jesus' own crucifixion and death lie in the immediate future. Risking his own life to give new life to Lazarus does not surprise us about Jesus. That is why he came into the world—to give new life to the human family, through his own death *and* resurrection. (April 5, 1992)

Loving God, I believe that Jesus is the resurrection and the life. Help me to be the instrument of your healing love so that others may experience new life and live in the circle of your mercy and love.

The Spirit of God calls us forth from our graves . . .
In God's Spirit, we *can* call each other from out of our
self-made graves. Let us first be aware of where our
corpses lie. Our self-made graves are everywhere. We
make graves in our high schools, our work and party
places, and in all our gathering spots. We make graves
whenever and wherever we blast away at the people on
the fringes, the oddballs and wounded birds. There is a
proverb that says that the most perfect weapon is the
human tongue, because it can kill another without
spilling a drop of blood. How many graves have we
filled through the practiced violence of our mocking
put-downs?

We make graves on our streets, in back alleys, in
parking lots and playgrounds—anyplace where we re-
sort to physical conflict to resolve interpersonal differences. We make graves whenever we decide that the
best way to change a person's mind is to bash in his
head. We make graves whenever we confuse muscle
with machismo and might with right. Physical violence
in all its forms has always made a multitude of graves.

We make graves out of relationships through stud-
ied or deliberate indifference. When we blind our eyes

to each other, we disengage our hearts. How many of us have bailed out on parent-family relationships, reducing our contact with them to the barest and coldest minimum? How many of us have cut ourselves off from the poor and suffering, isolating ourselves from any sense of connection and responsibility? How many of us have let prejudice kill any possibility of openness to an entire ethnic, national, or racial group? How many of us refuse to see the person behind the appearance, the living, breathing human being beneath the stereotype—be it preppie, jock, greaser, druggie, tramp, or rah-rah? We make graves out of relationships when we run and hide. . . .

Like the Marines, God is looking for a few good people. . . . Like an arrow, God aims himself at our hearts. Let us literally be peacemakers. It is through our concrete and real peace*making* that we will call each other from out of our self-made graves. . . . In God's Spirit, call each other from all your self-made graves. Be strong, not with the strength of the brute or the cynic but with the strength of the spark of God. Where there is isolation and interpersonal insulation, work to build community. Where people are dismissed and cut out on the basis of appearance, stereotype, or prejudice, gather together on the basis of understanding, humor, and compassion. Make your . . . communities models of a peacemaking people. That is more important than any project you can plan. That is the agenda I would like you to set for yourselves. (April 8, 1984)

God of life, send your Spirit to call me forth from the darkness of the graves I have created for myself. May the risen Lord help me spread peace, build bridges as a reconciler and honor the dignity of all persons.

JESUS IS RAISED
FROM THE DEAD

Pope John Paul II has said that the Stations of the Cross should end with a Fifteenth Station, Jesus' resurrection, because the paschal mystery ends not with Jesus' being buried in a tomb but rather with his resurrection, ascension, and the sending of the Holy Spirit.

Dying to self and rising to new life in Christ is a constant theme in Jesus' teaching. He has shown us the way, and God raised him from the dead after his crucifixion and burial. Because this is so important to the Christian faith, we celebrate Christ's resurrection every Sunday in a special way, even as we recall his death and resurrection at every celebration of the Eucharist. In Baptism we are also said to die to our old self and rise with the risen Lord to new life. The constant challenge is to live this new life each day.

Cardinal Bernardin built his spirituality on the promise and hope of the resurrection. When he celebrated the Eucharist at the Catholic Health Association meeting in Minneapolis on June 7, 1995, he already knew from his personal physician that he had an as yet unidentified health problem that could be quite serious. He underwent tests the very next day and learned that he had pancreatic cancer. Reading his hope-filled words about resurrection and new life on that occasion take on added significance, power and inspiration. Because he embraced the Cross and walked each painful mile of it with Jesus, he understood the resurrection

*as victory over death and as the power that imbues life with
its meaning.*

*The Way of the Cross is indeed the path to peace. It is
up to us to say yes to God's grace and embark on the awesome journey that leads us to encounter God in this world
and more intimately in the next.*

Brothers, I want to remind you of the gospel I
preached to you, which you received and in which
you stand firm. You are being saved by it at this
very moment if you hold fast to it as I preached
it to you. Otherwise you have believed in vain. I
handed on to you first of all what I myself received, that Christ died for our sins in accordance
with the Scriptures; that he was buried and, in accordance with the Scriptures, rose on the third day;
that he was seen by Cephas, then by the Twelve.
After that he was seen by five hundred brothers at
once, most of whom are still alive, although some
have fallen asleep. Next he was seen by James; then
by all the apostles. Last of all he was seen by me,
as one born out of the normal course. I am the
least of the apostles; in fact, because I persecuted
the church of God, I do not even deserve the
name. But by God's favor I am what I am. This

favor of his to me has not proved fruitless. Indeed, I have worked harder than all the others, not on my own but through the favor of God. In any case, whether it be I or they, this is what we preach and this is what you believed.

Tell me, if Christ is preached as raised from the dead, how is it that some of you say there is no resurrection of the dead? If there is no resurrection of the dead, Christ himself has not been raised. And if Christ has not been raised, our preaching is void of content and your faith is empty too. Indeed, we should then be exposed as false witnesses of God, for we have borne witness before him that he raised up Christ; but he certainly did not raise him up if the dead are not raised. Why? Because if the dead are not raised, then Christ was not raised; and if Christ was not raised, your faith is worthless. You are still in your sins, and those who have fallen asleep in Christ are the deadest of the dead. If our hopes in Christ are limited to this life only, we are the most pitiable of men.

(I CORINTHIANS 15:1–19)

Thanks to the death and resurrection of the Lord Jesus, death for the believer becomes a movement from life on this earth to greater life in heaven, from a veiled knowledge of God's love to the fullness of that love when we will see God face to face.

For those who try to respond to the call to love others as the Lord loved us, dying is, in a sense, an everyday occurrence in our lives. The Christian life is like a seed that has to fall to the ground, be buried, and broken open to produce fruit. Each of us needs to accept the daily difficulties and challenges of love, if the potential for life that God has created in us is to be realized.

We were baptized, Saint Paul says, into Jesus' death. That death was a dying to the old life to be able to rise to a new, better life. Through baptism we are "in Christ," and his spirit of life dwells in us. These truths will only seem real to us, however, if we try to deepen our awareness of the many ways in which the Lord is present to us as members of this believing community.

The difficulty, the dying, is the process of giving ourselves away. The Lord assures us in his love that each of us is precious and unique in his eyes. The life, which is ours, is his gift to us. Once we realize that, we know that we cannot keep his gift for ourselves. We must give ourselves to others. But this is not an easy task.

God's presence in our lives, however, energizes us and gives us hope. The Gospel's call to "hate" our lives in this world is an emphatic way of saying that true life is found only through rejecting those things that turn us from God, the source of life.

Too often, however, we become quite comfortable with the things that stand between God and us. As the Book of Wisdom says, "the witchery of paltry things obscures what is right and the whirl of desire transforms the innocent mind" (4:12). Turning away from things that have such a hold on us can be an uncomfortable kind of dying. But this is the only way to the fullness of life. So accepting the dying that leads to true life is something we do each day as believers. What we are really searching for each day is Christ himself, who says,
"Where I am,
there will my servant be"
(John 12:26).

We take up the challenges—the dying—of our baptism as soon as we step out of church. How does what we profess and experience *here* make sense in the world out *there*? Or, perhaps, we should turn the question around: How does the world out *there* make sense when we hear God's word and worship him in *here*?

We need to help one another find answers to these questions. We need to help one another build bridges and make connections that reconcile the world to Christ. In fact, we ourselves must become the connecting links. Our mission is to be ambassadors who show Christ to the world and help to make the world a new creation in his image.

But ambassadors need to have an intimate knowledge of the one they are representing. Ambassadors speak on behalf of others. So they need to know well the thoughts, demands, wishes, and points of view of those they represent.

That means that we need to know how to experience and celebrate Christ, the one whom we represent, in nature, in people, in the Scriptures, in the Eucharist, in moments of prayer and reflection. Our gatherings as a parish community are meant to help us to do this and to grow as representatives of the Lord in our world. (November 1, 1986)

Almighty God, I tend to hold on to things and peo-
ple. I want to control my own life. It is difficult for
me to "let go" of pet peeves and pet projects. It is
hard to "let go" of old habits and walk more
steadily and faithfully in your ways. Help me to
die to self so I may become the person you
created me to be.

United with Jesus in Love,
We Never Walk Alone

Jesus' promise—that he will never abandon us, that he
will not leave us orphans (John 14:18)—is not theoretical, pious, or superficial. It is real. It is living. And, my
dear brothers and sisters, it is made to you and me!

This passage from Saint John's Gospel occurs at the
Last Supper when Jesus is saying good-bye to his disciples. We can imagine their inner tension, their bitter-
sweet anxiety, their fear of being abandoned—lost
without Jesus. They need to be reassured. So Jesus
prays that his disciples—not only those in the Upper
Room but also his disciples for all ages to come—will
love him and remain united to him, just as he is one
with the Father.

"If you love me
and obey the commands I give
you" [Jesus said], "I will ask the Father
and he will give you another Paraclete—
to be with you always:
the Spirit of truth."

(JOHN 14:15–16)

Jesus is saying, in effect, "When you are united with me in love, I will never—I can never—abandon you. You will never be orphans! You will never stand or walk alone!"

Even though the risen Lord now dwells at God's right hand, his Holy Spirit, his special gift to the community of faith, is still wonderfully accessible to us today.

. . . Although we are not witnesses to the risen Lord in precisely the same way as Peter and the other disciples, we have experienced foretastes of the resurrection, we have experienced the presence of Jesus in our lives in so many ways. Let me explain what I mean.

Our ability to survive and keep trusting after the death of a loved one or after we have experienced some other psychological trauma; our passage from ignorance, bias, and intellectual narrowness to greater insight, broader acceptance, and more openness; our human capacity to hope and to protest human misery and suffering, despite the prevalence of defeatism and cynicism; our willingness to dedicate our lives to serving others despite the frequent obstacles and setbacks we encounter—all of these are partial foretastes of the experience of the resurrection. They point to the fullness of life, meaning, and love that Jesus himself shared with us at Easter. They remind us that the risen Lord is always present among us.

[The] gospel challenges us to allow our lives to be transformed by that plenitude of meaning and love, to live out the implications of the new life inaugurated by the Easter mysteries.

If you have ever fallen in love, moving from an overconcern about yourself to a greater concern for someone else, you have experienced new life. Jesus asks us to love as he loves: Love the sick, the elderly, the forgotten, the oppressed, the addicted, the marginal people.

If you have ever moved beyond hopelessness, despair, or cynicism to discover meaning and an abiding goodness in life, you have experienced Easter; you have experienced the presence of the risen Lord. And Jesus asks us today to be instruments of peace and sacraments of hope for those who have neither the power nor the experience of either.

If your life has ever been revitalized or renewed, if you have ever been given a second chance to undo past mistakes, if you have ever been given a new lease on life after suffering from a physical, emotional, or spiritual trauma, you have experienced resurrection. Jesus asks us today to share with others the Good News that has been proclaimed to us, the wonderful realities that we have personally enjoyed.

We need to pay close attention to these experiences of new life, for we are often besieged by the counter-forces of violence, chaos, and death. In his letter to the Romans, Saint Paul defines this human condition in cosmic proportions. He speaks of all creation groaning expectantly for the fullness of salvation when the human family will finally live in communion with God and the whole of creation of good will yearn to be free of the restraint of corruption that sin places upon us [Romans 8:18–25].

For Saint Paul, hope is the trademark of a committed Christian, but not the kind of hope that is mere wishful thinking. Hope is not a naïve optimism that tries, without any credible basis, to persuade us that things will inevitably get better. No, our hope is based on the risen Lord's abiding presence among us and on the gift of his Holy Spirit. And on the basis of this hope, and our trust in this divine presence, we walk on our pilgrim journey and carry out our ministry with confidence, courage, and inner peace.

. . . And that is why we gather around the eucharistic table. We gather in the presence of the risen Lord. We have listened to the word of God. And we partake of Jesus' body and blood, which will nourish and strengthen us for our pilgrim journey and our ministry of healing. By shedding his own blood, Jesus revealed that our true greatness—indeed, our authentic vocation—is to share the gift of ourselves with others, especially the most vulnerable in our society. As Pope John Paul II has pointed out,

> Precisely because it is poured out as the gift of life, the blood of Christ is no longer a sign of death . . . but the instrument of a communion which is richness of life for all. Whoever in the sacrament of the Eucharist . . . drinks this blood and abides in Jesus . . . is drawn into the dynamism of his love and gift of life, in order to bring to its fullness the original vocation to love which belongs to everyone.
>
> (*EVANGELIUM VITAE*, 25)

My friends, the Eucharist establishes a communion of life between ourselves and the Lord and among ourselves. His is an awesome mystery! . . . My prayer for all of us is that we continue to grow in the experience and living-out of Easter. May we open our minds and hearts so Jesus and his Father and the Holy Spirit may always dwell within us. (June 7, 1995)

> *God of all consolation, the death and resurrection*
> *of your beloved Son have changed the human fam-*
> *ily forever. My Christian hope is based on the risen*
> *Lord's abiding presence in my life and in that of*
> *my community—indeed, throughout the world.*
> *Based on that hope, may I walk on my pilgrim way*
> *with all my brothers and sisters, confident that you*
> *love me and all of us very, very much.*

JOSEPH LOUIS BERNARDIN served as Archbishop of Cincinnati and President of the National Conference of Catholic Bishops in Washington, D.C. He became a Cardinal in 1983 and was Archbishop of Chicago from 1982 until his death in 1996. Widely recognized as both a church and civic leader, he was awarded the Medal of Freedom shortly before he died.

ALPHONSE P. SPILLY, C.PP.S., served as special assistant to Cardinal Bernardin from 1984 to 1996. He assisted with *The Gift of Peace* and edited the two-volume *Selected Works of Joseph Cardinal Bernardin*. He is director of the Joseph Cardinal Bernardin Center for Theology and Ministry at the Catholic Theological Union in Chicago.

JEREMY LANGFORD edited *The Gift of Peace* and two biographical photobooks of the Cardinal by John H. White, *This Man Bernardin* and *The Final Journey of Joseph Cardinal Bernardin*. He is editor-in-chief of Sheed & Ward Book Publishing and is earning a master's degree as a Bernardin scholar at the Catholic Theological Union in Chicago.